the sculptor's handbook

**Series Consultant Editors:
Stan Smith and
Professor H.F. Ten Holt**

MACDONALD & CO
LONDON & SYDNEY

Contents

the
sculptor's
handbook

A QED BOOK

Copyright ©1984 QED Publishing Limited
First published in Great Britain in 1984 by
Macdonald & Co (Publishers) Ltd
London & Sydney

Maxwell House
74 Worship Street, London EC2A 2EN

ISBN 0 356 10573 3

This book was designed and produced by
QED Publishing Limited
32 Kingly Court
London W1

Printed by Leefung Asco Printers Limited,
Hong Kong

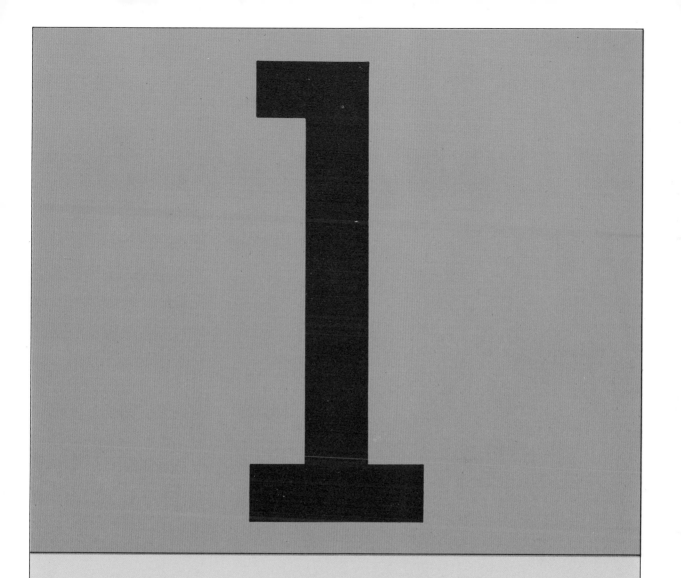

Design principles in sculpture.

Elements of design: Mass, Space, Plane, Line, Movement, Scale, Texture, Colour.

Sculpture Design Principles

S culpture has no clearly defined boundaries, and a dictionary definition states that it is the act of carving, especially in stone, extended to clay modelling or moulding for casting. The twentieth century, however, has seen this definition extended to include any media, so that a sculpture may now consist of an arrangement of bricks or a huge curtain suspended across a canyon. Such works demand that the spectator should take an active role in the interpretation of the work, and this is the aim of many modern sculptors.

The concept of a sculpture must relate to the medium, and whether working figuratively or in an abstract form this sense of balance or respect for the medium should not be ignored.

Although Rodin (1840–1917) heeded formal values, his chief concern was with nature, rather than with art, and the expression of character and movement: 'Conceive form in depth. Clearly indicate the dominant planes. Imagine forms as directed towards you; all life surges from a centre, expands from within outwards. In drawing, observe relief not outline. The relief determines the contour. The main thing is to be moved, to love, to hope, to tremble, to live. Be a man before being an artist!'

Constructivist artists sought to explore and exploit the aesthetic, physical and functional capacities of materials while researching the basic elements of space, volume and colour. Although constructivist works lead towards the abstract, Naum Gabo (1890–1977), one of the pioneers, claimed that: '... abstract is not the core of the Constructive ideal. The idea means more to me. It involves the whole complex of human relation to life. It is a mode of thinking, acting, perceiving and living... Any thing or action that enhances life, propels it and adds to it something in the direction of growth, expansion and development is constructive.'

These two viewpoints alone demonstrate that sculpture cannot be viewed as a collection of formal principles.

More recently, Carl Andre (born 1935) has produced work which has attempted to confront the spectator with forms in which inherent significance is minimal. He has summarized his artistic evolution from his early wood sculptures, to his stacking of wood units, to his floor pieces as passing from form to structure to place. Such a development expresses a move away from all representational values to a concern with producing sculptures that allow the spectator to view an object devoid of built-in significance and therefore capable of reinterpretation. Such works should not be confused with the abstract.

Contemporary sculpture differs from the work of previous centuries for many reasons. These include a decreased preoccupation with the human body used as a subject to convey ideas, the development of constructivist processes and the use of modern materials and techniques, the use of colour, and changing attitudes to artistic achievement.

The twentieth century has seen the emergence of sculptors who have examined images from many other cultures and this has served to widen a vocabulary which has been almost exclusively related to Greek ideals. Rodin's work breathed new life into sculpture, and artists such as Brancusi (1876–1957), Picasso (1881–1973), Gabo and Tatlin (1885–1953) have helped create new ground into which sculpture has now extended.

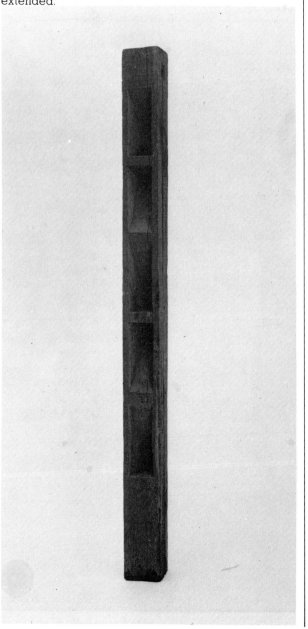

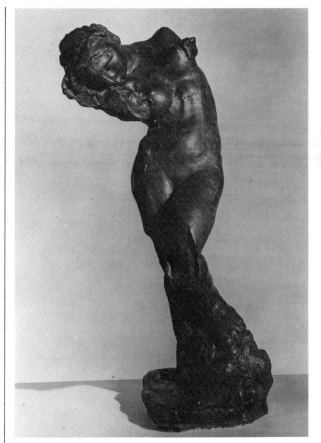

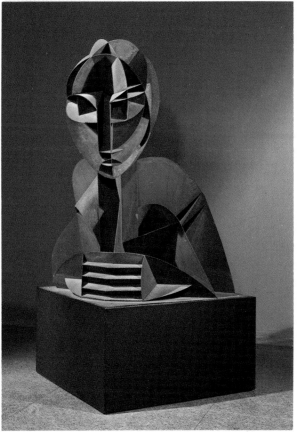

Changing forms in sculpture
Until the end of the nineteenth
century, sculptors were largely
preoccupied with representations
of the human form in their work. In
this century, abstract concepts of
structure and the development of
new materials for sculptors have
broadened the range of attitudes
towards the design and execution
of a sculpture. Rodin's *The Muse*
(**above**) shows that he was already
beginning to abandon a strict
representation of a body in favour
of a more tactile, personal
impression of the form. The
beginnings of truly abstract
sculpture appear in the work of the
Cubists and Constructivists, as
shown by Naum Gabo's
interpretation of the traditional
portrait bust, *Head* (**above right**).
Picasso's painting and sculpture
helped to change attitudes, and
his Cubist reliefs, such as this *Still
Life* (**right**), explored the territory
between painting and sculpture,
transposing some of his ideas first
expressed in paint into three-
dimensional form. More recently,
the nature of the sculptor's
materials has to some extent
become the subject of the work, as
in minimal sculptures such as Carl
Andre's *Last Ladder* (**left**).

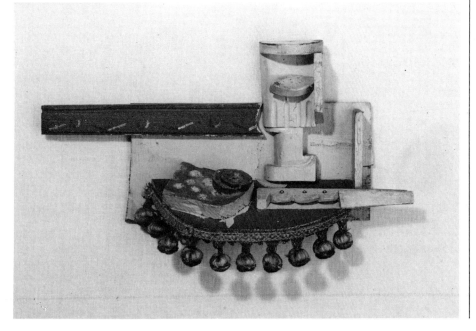

Sculpture Elements of design

ertain basic elements in sculptural work can be pinpointed: elements, such as mass, scale, line and texture, can extend and realize an idea in conjunction with the medium used.

Mass

This element has always been foremost in the presentation of sculpture. The traditional materials of sculpture, stone and bronze, and their associated techniques make the consideration of volume essential.

Sculptures with a clarity of surface, presenting strong, clear profiles, allow their three-dimensional quality to be comprehended visually. A surface that is highly modelled reflects light in such a way that the solidity or apparent weight of the sculpture is diminished.

Rodin's work is concerned essentially with light and movement in comparison with that of Maillol (1861–1944) which uses the weight and balance of mass to greater effect.

It is advisable to avoid using masses with the same volume in a single work unless conscious repetition and symmetry are desired.

Space

If two related forms are placed next to each other and then slowly moved apart, the space between them changes both in dimension and character. When the two forms are close together the intervening space may seem restricted, whereas when the forms are separated the space may become less tense but it still relates to both forms. If the forms are moved even further apart, they will read as two separate, unrelated forms and the space that was once a part of the sculpture becomes space surrounding those separate forms.

Interaction between space and mass is perhaps best demonstrated in the work of Henry Moore (born 1898). The surface of a mass touches space where the inner tensions of a form are countered, and Moore, by allowing space to penetrate mass, emphasizes this balance.

Plane

A plane is generally considered to be an element that has two dimensions, length and width. The thickness of a plane in sculpture must be minimal in relation to the other elements in order to differentiate between plane and volume.

A plane can be curved or straight and this will affect the way that it is read. The materials usually used bend or fold on only one axis at a time, but those such as plastics and sheet metal can be bent in two directions at once.

From one viewpoint the edge of a plane will read as a line: if, for example, a piece of paper is torn so that it has a ragged edge, the line formed by that edge appears from one view to have a kind of movement in space; from the view at right angles to the first, however, it reads as a line, either straight or curved, and it will have a different relationship to the space through which it moves.

Line

A form or plane can be suggested by line, and line can give a sculpture a sense of space. Vertical lines are associated with support and strength and can give a work a monumental quality. They support structures both physically and visually, whereas the horizontal elements are themselves supported and are more passive. A diagonal line tends to be more active than either a vertical or a horizontal because its inclination to the ground creates tensions which are not familiar. A line, which can be straight, curved or flowing, can be created with string, wire or rods, tensioned between points.

The type of line, its length, the material used and its relationship to other parts of the sculpture create dynamics which affect the interpretation of the work. A convex line, for example, is active in creating tensions, while a concave line appears to be subjected to implied or real forces.

Movement

Sculptors have for centuries produced images with implied movement. Rodin achieved a sense of motion not only by concentrating on poses in mid-movement but by the use of surface modelling, a process that produces a work capable of interaction with light.

Because of their lack of mass, figures sculpted by Giacometti (1901–1966) give the surrounding space a tremendous vibration, as though they are about to move and occupy the space in which they stand.

Alexander Calder (1898–1976) used real movement in his work: his mobiles respond both to the movement of the spectator and the environmental air currents.

It is preferable not to place a sculpture on a revolving base, unless such movement is an integral part of the work, as the spectator should always be able to view the work at his or her own pace and from whichever angle he or she chooses.

When mechanical and electronic movement are used in sculpture, the power source and mechanization is best considered as part of the work.

Scale

This is an essential element to be considered in all sculpture. A sculpture developed through maquettes may need to change as the size increases, as different elements in the composition assert themselves. Mass, for instance, is an element that needs size to make an impact. Sculptures that relate to the human scale are generally better suited to confined areas than monumental works. Monumental sculptures are best exhibited outdoors where they can be seen as part of their environment.

Texture

The varying textures and finishes of sculptural media can be worked to create shadow, or reduce or heighten the reflective qualities of the surface. A heavy texture, produced for example in carving a block of stone, may be used as the final surface so as to create shadow or emphasize the weight. The same texture on a bronze work, owing to its reflective qualities, may destroy the visual weight of the work.

A highly polished surface on a bronze may use light to modify the mass, whereas a highly polished white marble may deaden the image—and this has led to the frequent use of coloured or figured stone.

David Smith (1906–1965) has used a grinder on his stainless steel constructions which helps to integrate his sculptures with their environment: the surface absorbs the surrounding colours and light while not reflecting images itself, and thus it keeps the volumes of the work intact.

The techniques used often suggest the finish. Adding texture to a sculpture at the end of the process may mean that the work lacks inherent sculptural value, and this demands a re-examination of the piece or the materials used.

Colour

Sculpture often uses the natural colours of the materials. Stone may have a wax polish applied to reveal the true colour of its figuring, and wood is often waxed to emphasize the grain. Patinas are frequently applied to bronze sculptures to age the work and to reduce its reflective surface.

Modern sculptors have tended to keep the natural finish of the materials they use especially when working with steel, concrete, wood and stone. Steel sculptures can be made from rusty stock, the surface being retained in the final work.

Wood, metal and plastic sculptures, especially, can be painted both to unify a work of several components and for protection. As paint obscures the natural surface, the spectator is forced to read the sculpture in terms of its lines of direction, movement and colour. Thought should be given to the work when deciding whether to use gloss, matt, glazed or polychromed paints. The use of more than one colour may draw attention only to the surface of the work, but it can also delineate separate rhythms or elements.

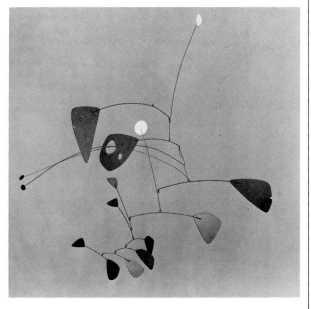

Movement in sculpture The problems of expressing movement in sculpture have to some extent been solved by Kinetic sculpture, in which part or all of the work actually moves. This is quite a recent development and the attempts to imply movement in essentially static objects have given rise to a number of styles of work over the years. The thin, spare figures created by Giacometti, such as *Man Pointing* (**right**), create a considerable impression of mobility, both in their gestures, and in the figures or groups of figures as a whole. Alexander Calder has been one of the most consistent experimenters in the field of moving sculpture, producing a variety of mobiles and power driven sculptures. *Antennae with Red and Blue Dots* (**above**), a typical example of his mobiles, highlights another feature of his work, the use of different coloured elements in the composition.

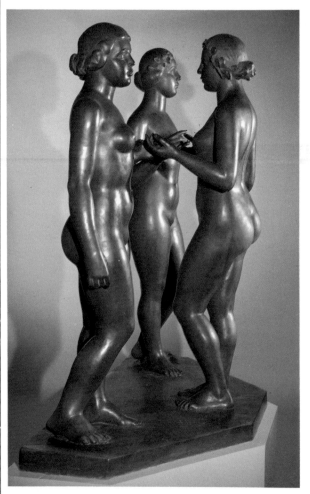

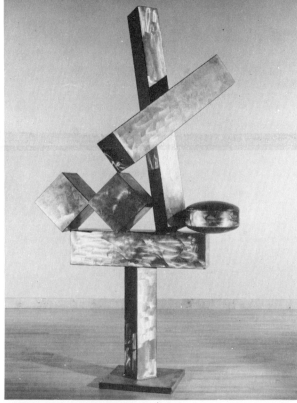

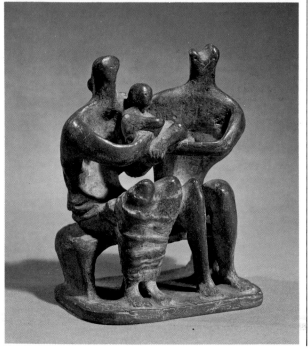

Weight, volume and balance
Until the open structure of modern metal and transparent plastic sculptures evolved, the traditional preoccupations of the sculptor were the volume and mass of an object produced by techniques of carving and modelling. Stone, clay, plaster and bronze all have an unavoidable weight and substance which is part of their very nature, and the sheer physical effort of making a sculpture has been noted by many artists throughout history. Modern techniques of welding and construction have opened up the possibility of overcoming a great many of the physical problems involved in translating an initial design into three-dimensional form, as can be seen in David Smith's *Cubi XIX* (**above right**). This is one of a series of sculptures in which the weight of the material elements seems denied by the precarious balancing of the component parts and by the way in which a solid form can extend into open space. In earlier sculptures, the extension of the forms was limited by the block of stone in carving, or by the balance and structure of the supportive armature in modelling. As can be seen in Maillol's *Three Nymphs* (**above left**), the gestures of the figures were often restrained and there is a very different attitude to balance and symmetry from that in Smith's work. The solidity of the figures is notable, relieved only by the spaces between them incorporated in the grouping. *Maquette for Family Group* by Henry Moore (**right**) is a sculpture which clearly demonstrates his ability to combine traditional principles of form and structure with his own innovations. The pose of the group and his respect for the qualities of his materials show his roots in a long tradition of figure sculpture, but the distortion of the figures in the altered scale and form of the limbs, bodies and heads are characteristic of his personal approach.

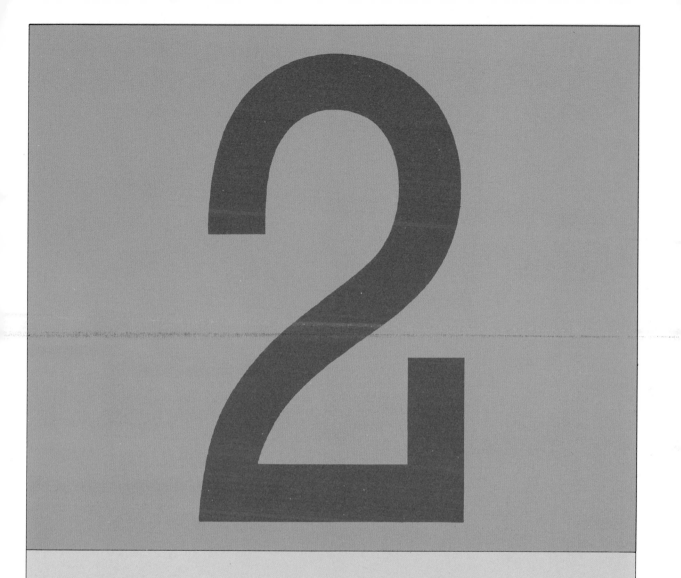

Carving stone.

History. Types of stone: Alabaster, Granite, Limestone, Marble, Sandstone, Slate, Soapstone. **Techniques:** Selection, Sawing a block, Boasting and roughing-out, Shaping, Developing, Finishing, Waxing, Making a plaster block for carving, Carving granite, Safety precautions. **Equipment:** Power tools, Carving tools, Finishing tools.

Stone-carving History

S tones may be divided into three categories: igneous, sedimentary, or metamorphic rock. Igneous rock is formed by the cooling and recrystallization of molten materials in the earth. They are usually extremely hard, even textured and very durable.

The ancient Egyptians were prolific carvers, and for almost 3,000 years their style hardly changed. Both hard and soft stone were used, including granite and limestone. The softer sculptures, including the great Sphinx of Giza, were coated with gypsum before the vivid colours, which the Egyptians used on all stone-carving, were applied. Female statues were usually painted yellow and males dark red. Clothes were depicted in bright colours and eyes were often shown by white quartz with a coloured iris.

Historians have relied heavily on the stone-carvings found in ancient Assyria and Babylon, later part of Mesopotamia, for clues to these early civilizations. Marble and stone statues and reliefs excavated from ruined temples and palaces have shown in detail the traditions and costume of people who lived more than 2,000 years ago. Some of the carvings were executed in diorite, one of the hardest and most difficult stones to carve. One of the most notable surviving examples is the statue of Gudea of Lagash, now in the Louvre.

It was not until the fifth century BC in Greece that stone-carving, freed from religious dictates, became an art form. Much of the work was done in marble, the Parthenon statues being the best known examples of the liberated, life-like style. This 'Golden Age', as it is sometimes called, produced most of the classical carving which has had a profound and lasting influence upon sculptors.

Roman stone-carvers initially imitated the Greeks, whose work they greatly admired. By the first and second centuries AD however, when much of the civilized world was part of the Roman Empire, the Romans had developed a realistic, aggressive style of their own. Their marble and stone statues and busts were true to life, and never idealized or flattering. Like the Greeks, the Romans painted stone statues, probably in vivid colours.

After the fall of the Roman Empire, during the period known as the Dark Ages, all the arts suffered a decline. Early Christian crosses, depicting biblical figures and vine-patterns, are almost the only examples of stone-carving to have survived from this bleak period.

Pre-Columbian peoples, such as the Totonac on the Gulf Coast of America (200–900 AD), sculpted monumental stelae from local rock, and later the great temples and palaces of Aztec Mexico, built between 1325 and 1520, were adorned with carved sculptures of the gods.

In the twelfth century the heavy carving of early Christian art gave way to the lighter, Gothic style. Although carving was regarded as an extension of architecture, there is an abundance of carved statues, decoration and gargoyles to be found on churches of this time. Such carvings, though lacking the proportion and perfection of classical works, were usually well observed and often satirical. Stone-carving gradually separated from masonry and became an art form in its own right.

During the Italian Renaissance marble was by far the most popular stone, and the revival of the classical ideals of Greek art, which reached its peak during the High Renaissance (c.1500–1527), exerted a widespread influence on sculpture.

The Italian sculptor, Gianlorenzo Bernini (1598–1680), was the greatest exponent of Baroque carving, a style which emerged during the late sixteenth century. His work in stone and marble excels in absolute detail, and his naturalistic approach rejected many of the ideals of the Renaissance.

The classical tradition, however, continued its influence for the next 300 years. There was often conflict between classicists and artists such as the Frenchman Auguste Rodin (1840–1917), who preferred to express more natural forms.

Much twentieth-century carving has moved away from the representational approach completely. Two British sculptors have played a major role in this. Henry Moore (born 1898) was one of the first to place a greater emphasis on the development of form than on imitation of the subject. Barbara Hepworth (1903–1975), carving directly in stone, was a totally non-figurative sculptor.

The variety of stone and fabricated carving materials plays an important role in sculpture. Although in many respects stone is still used in the same architectural context as it was in Greece, as demonstrated in the works of American sculptor, Isamu Noguchi (born 1904), whose works in marble and granite can be seen throughout the United States, and in the monumental works of the Swiss sculptor, Hans Aeschbacher (born 1906). The scope of the stone-carver today is broader and has resulted in an enormous diversity of approach among the thousands of modern stone-carvers.

Despite this diversity, stone-carving remains a very traditional sculpture medium. Just as the actual materials have changed little over the centuries, so the basic stone-carvers tools have not changed fundamentally. Technological developments have, however, provided the sculptor with tools made of better quality metal, and have made available power tools which are particularly useful for cutting large pieces of stone.

The actual techniques of stone-carving have also changed relatively little; it is how they are used which has changed in the twentieth century. In stone-carving, as in painting, this century has seen the rise of the abstract. While in painting this has tended to be accompanied by a parallel expansion in the artist's technical repertoire, in stone-carving the techniques of centuries have been used to create the new and different forms.

Most stones can be worked in accordance with the following techniques, but granite requires slightly different methods which are described later. It should be noted that choice of stone is just as important as mastering the basic techniques.

Sedimentary rock is made up of tiny particles of stone which have at some stage been deposited in water where they have combined with bone remains and other calcium carbonate substances. They are more porous than igneous rocks, are softer and easier to carve and give a textured, rather than a polished finish. Limestone and sandstone both belong to this group.

Metamorphic rock is igneous or sedimentary rock which has been transformed by heat, pressure, or some other force in the earth's crust. These types of rock are usually soft to carve and include marble, alabaster, slate and soapstone.

The most durable and weather-resistant types of stone are granites and other igneous rocks. Very porous stone is less suitable for carvings intended to stand outdoors, especially in damp conditions where water can freeze in the stone and gradually cause the stone to disintegrate. Wind, sand and dust are all harmful to stone over a period of time, and many urban pollutions, such as soot, are erosive.

Alabaster
Used in ancient Egypt and the Middle East and extensively in Europe in the later Middle Ages, alabaster is a fine-grained, smooth and translucent stone. It is soft and easy to work, and can produce a high finish. It is available in many translucent and pastel shades of yellow or pink as well as white and clear. Alabaster is easily scratched, and is most suited to small sculptures and work protected from the weather.

Granite
It was used in ancient Egypt for many monuments including the Luxor obelisk and Cleopatra's Needle (now on the Victoria Embankment, London). As it is an extremely hard and durable stone, granite is often used for outdoor sculptures. It has a rather rough texture and contains particles of spar and crystal which give polished granite a reflective quality in bright light. Porphyry granite, a specially hard type because of its high spar content, is a particular favourite for its distinctive sparkling quality in light. Granite is not suitable for detailed carving and is usually used for large works. It is difficult to work and requires special tools. The stone has to be pulverized and bruised before chiselling. Colours range from yellow, rose, green and most commonly from light grey through black. It is capable of a very high finish.

Limestone
The texture and colour of limestone, a sedimentary rock composed essentially of carbonate of lime, vary greatly, depending on its origin. Textures range from the easily worked and quickly weathered lias and freestone to the fine-grained oolites, some of which weather well and can be carved with precision. Grey and beige are the most common colours, but pink and green varieties exist too. One of the best limestones for carving is the fine, close-textured Caen limestone from France which has been used extensively by the British artist Henry Moore.

Marble
The greatest Greek sculptors used marble, and it is the traditional favourite of stone-carvers. The infinite variety of colours and colour combinations depends on where it is quarried. Marble is found in many countries including America, Canada, France and Greece. Belgian Tournai marble is hard and black and much favoured by sculptors today. Italian marble is one of the best available, notably the Carrara marble used by Michelangelo. Marble is characteristically easy to carve and takes a fine, glossy polish.

Sandstone
The Egyptians used sandstone from the earliest times, and it was used extensively in England in the Middle Ages and for Cologne Cathedral in Germany which was begun in 1248. The quality of sandstone as a carving material depends largely upon the amount of quartz it contains. If there is no quartz the stone breaks and splinters easily, but too much quartz makes it difficult to carve. Sandstone comes in many colours, depending on the nature of the sand and the cementing matter. The colours include browns, reds, greys and greenish hues. It is generally rather porous and, like limestone, takes a poor finish. Some varieties are insufficiently weather-resistant.

Slate
Although it has a tendency to split, slate is valued for its availability, its high finish and its weather-resistant properties. It is usually blue-black or blue-grey.

Soapstone
Sometimes called steatite, soapstone is a very soft, smooth stone like marble, but with a soapy texture. Its softness and ready availability make it a particularly useful stone for beginners. Soapstone is usually a dull green or a bluish grey, or sometimes brown. It can be used only for indoor sculptures because of its vulnerability in damp conditions.

Other materials for the stone-carver
Less traditional materials for the modern stone-carver include many inexpensive building materials. Different types of concrete blocks, aerated concrete, bricks, chalk and plaster of Paris have all been carved and worked successfully.

Cement and concrete are available in numerous sizes, colours and textures. Although they are generally not suited to detailed work, bricks and blocks have been used for relief carving, assembled structures and small free-standing works. Aerated concrete is particularly easy to carve.

Blocks of plaster of Paris are cheap and effective for rapid, detailed work, and they can be carved either with special tools or with knives, blades and nail files.

The work can be coloured with water or oil paints, inks or dyes, and can be easily sealed with a coat of colourless shoe polish.

A lump of chalk, being soft and easy to work, can make good carving material, although it may be necessary to scrape off the weathered outer layer. It is similar to plaster, and it can be carved and coloured as described above.

Types of stone There are three main categories of stone — igneous, sedimentary and metamorphic. Limestone (**2**) and sandstone (**1**) are both sedimentary rocks. These are relatively soft, easy to carve and give a textured rather than a polished finish. Slate, such as Welsh slate (**3**) or Westmorland slate (**4**) and marble (**5**) are examples of metamorphic rock, and are also fairly easy to carve. The hardest type of rock is igneous. Granite is the best known example of this category. Granite comes in a wide variety of colours and textures including Emerald Pearl from Norway (**6**), South African grey (**7**), Cornish (**9**). Balmoral (**10**) and Karin (**8**) both come from Scotland. Granite, which is difficult to carve and needs special hard tools, is suitable for carvings which will stand outside because it is a very durable stone. Other stones such as aerated concrete (**11**) and brick (**12**) can also be put to good use by the stone-carver. One of the softer stones is best for the beginner to work with. It is vital to master basic techniques before embarking on either a large scale work or on a carving in one of the harder stones.

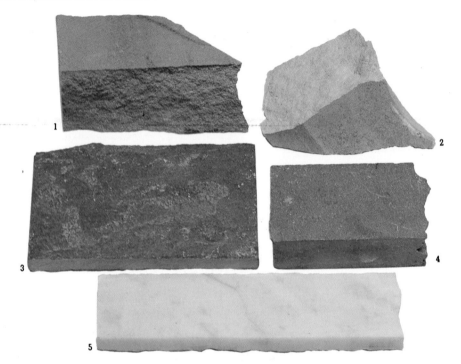

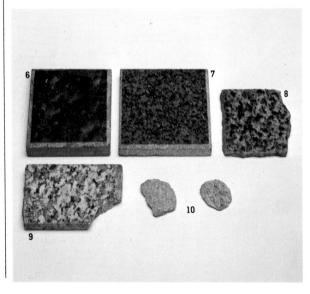

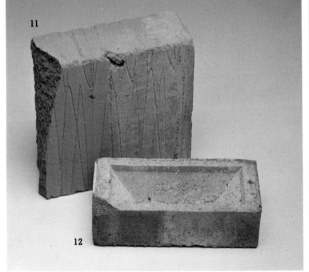

Stone-carving Tools and equipment

With the exception of the hammers, which are made of iron, stone-carving tools are forged from tempered steel. Tools used for granite-carving are especially hard and often have tungsten carbide tips.

Boasting and roughing-out
Boucharde Sometimes known as a bush hammer, the boucharde has V-shaped indentations and is used for bruising and pulverizing the stone to soften it. This technique is used particularly with very hard stones such as granite. The boucharde must not be used in the final stages as dull marks will show through to the surface of the stone.

Hammer The stone-carver's hammer usually weighs between 2-2½lbs (about 1kg) for stones of average hardness, but they can be much lighter or as heavy as 4lbs (about 2kg), depending on the type of work being done.

Pitcher This is a large heavy implement used with the hammer to remove large lumps of stone in the early stages.

Point Variously sized points are used to remove waste stone. A good carver removes waste stone to within a very small distance of the finished shape using points.

Shaping
Claw This chisel-type tool has teeth and produces a cross-hatching effect. Much of the rough modelling is done with the claw. Claws designed specially for marble-carving have longer teeth.

Chisel The carving is developed with chisels and gouges which come in different sizes with variously shaped cutting edges.

Mallet The stone-carver's mallet, usually made of a hard wood such as beechwood, is used mainly for soft stone, and can be used in conjunction with any mallet-headed tool, such as a chisel, for finer work.

Rasps, files and rifflers These are used in the final stages of the carving to give a smooth finish, for final modelling, and to eliminate the marks made by the claw and the chisels.

Power tools
A variety of electric or pneumatic tools are suitable for carving and shaping stone for sculpture. Pneumatic tools are especially effective for carving hard stone.

Carving
Chisels and gouges Claws, chisels and gouges are available in all sizes to fit power tools. Power carving saves time, but very great care must be taken not to fracture the stone.

Drill Carbide tips are required when drilling stone.

Hammer Electric hammers are less adaptable than pneumatic hammers, the latter being heavier and more effective with hard stone.

Saws Power saws are essential for cutting stone blocks. Special masonry blades are used and it is often necessary to pour water over both stone and blade during cutting to reduce friction and heat.

Finishing
Body grinder Although usually used for metal work, the body grinder can be fitted with a masonry wheel and is very time-saving for finishing large sculptures.

Electric sander This is excellent for finishing and polishing large areas. It can be fitted with all grades of abrasive papers and with a buffer attachment for the final polishing.

Stone-carving tools and equipment Equipment for preparing the stone includes a saw (**4**), mason's hammers (**8**), tape-measure (**7**), dividers (**12**) and adjustable set-square (**9**). The stone is roughed out using the boaster (**18**) and worked with the points (**14**), claws (**16**), flats (**17**) and smaller chisels (**15**). The stone is brushed at intervals during carving with a wire brush (**10**). The stone is smoothed further with the files, beginning with the coarse stone file (**11**) and then the finer two-sided files which come in a wide variety of sizes and shapes (**13**). The stone is finished with different grades of carborundum stone (**6**) and silicon carbide paper (**5**). The finished stone can be waterproofed with a coat of silicon liquid (**2**). A bucket (**3**) is useful for wetting the stone at various stages, and the tools can be kept in a bag (**1**).

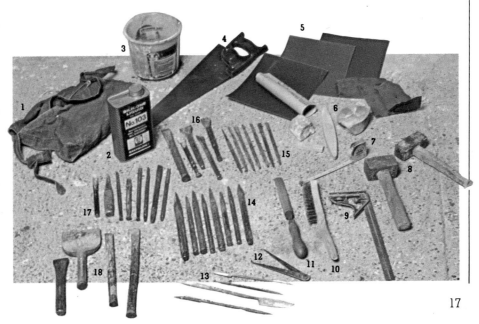

The basic tool kit

A metal hammer weighing between 2–2½lbs (about 1kg), a pitcher and two or three variously sized points are essential for roughing-out. The next stages require a selection of claws with teeth of different sizes and different spacing and an assortment of chisels and gouges, depending on the size and type of carving. A range of abrasive papers for polishing and appropriate filing tools for smoothing are essentials.

The stone-carver's kit is completed with a pair of plastic goggles and a simple respirator for protection against flying chips and dust.

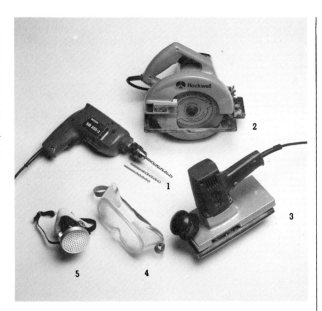

Power tools Power tools are useful for cutting through stone more quickly than is possible by hand. A drill with tungsten carbide bits (**1**) is particularly useful. The bits must be strong enough to cut through the stone, so tungsten carbide is recommended. When using a power saw (**2**), make sure that the blade is suitable for cutting through stone. The sander (**5**) can be used for polishing large surfaces. It is important when using power tools to wear goggles (**4**) and a respirator (**3**) to counteract the fine stone dust which the power tools create.

Stone-carving Techniques

S tone-carving both in art and architecture has existed for many thousands of years. Some of the earliest examples are limestone figurines, found in France during the late nineteenth century, which date back to the Stone Age.

Selection

Freshly quarried stone should be used whenever possible. Stone which has weathered usually has a hard outer crust which makes it difficult to carve.

Dry, rough stone never indicates the true colour of the stone. Wetting the surface will reveal the colour of the finished, polished stone.

Many pieces of stone and rock contain flaws, cracks or weak layers. Although these are sometimes visible, they are quite often hidden in what appears to be a perfectly sound specimen. Hidden faults can sometimes be detected by tapping the stone with a steel hammer. A sound stone produces a ringing tone, but a bad stone gives a dead, dull sound. A weak layer in a stone often turns darker than the rest when the entire stone is soaked in water.

Sawing a block

Hard stones and large stones are usually cut in a stone-cutter's yard with industrial equipment. Softer and smaller stones can be cut with a portable saw fitted with a special blade. Water should be poured over the blade at frequent intervals to prevent it overheating.

Boasting and roughing-out

These initial stages are accompanied with a pitcher and large points used with a metal hammer. Any large, simple areas of waste are cut with a saw, and the block is laid in position on several layers of burlap or non-slip mats. Holding the point at an oblique angle, the roughing-out is then carefully carried out, the edges and corners being worked first. The carving should be done in short parallel strokes at right angles to each other, creating a criss-cross pattern on the stone. This process removes the waste stone evenly and is continued until the rough shape is achieved. Surplus stone chippings are removed with a stiff brush.

Shaping

After the roughing-out, the first shaping is worked with the claws. The larger sizes are used first, working through to the finer tools. The same criss-cross motion of the roughing-out process should be maintained, giving the sculpture a fine cross-hatched surface.

Developing

The shape is developed using chisels or claws, depending on the detail and design of the sculpture.

Stone-carving: Techniques

After removing the criss-cross ridges with a flat chisel, further shaping can be carried out with rasps and files.

Finishing
Garnet paper or waterproof silicon carbide paper, known as wet-and-dry, is used to produce a smooth finish for polishing. The carving should be soaked first if possible, and must be kept wet all the time. The sediment which builds up during this process should be removed frequently. Starting with the coarsest papers and changing gradually to the finer grades, the surface is rubbed down until all the scratches and tool marks have disappeared. Wet-and-dry should be used wet, a small area being worked at a time. Emery paper or a fine emery cloth may be used after the wet-and-dry. Pumice or putty powder is sometimes applied with a wet pad and the carving rubbed well to produce a final finish. The surface can be polished finally with a dry cloth.

Making a plaster block for carving
Cardboard boxes, milk and fruit-juice cartons and many other containers are ideal moulds for making plaster of Paris blocks for carving. The correct amount of water is estimated by filling the mould almost to the top. The water is then poured into a mixing bowl and the dry plaster sprinkled over it until a small mound of plaster rises above the surface of the water. When mixed the plaster should be the consistency of a thick sauce. It is poured quickly into the mould, which should be greased with Vaseline or liquid soap to prevent sticking, and allowed to dry before the mould is removed.

Carving granite
Granite is harder than most other stones and it needs specially tempered tools; such tools are heavier than standard stone-carving tools and some have tungsten carbide tips.

The technique for carving granite is also slightly different: waste stone is removed by first being pulverized or bruised, with a granite axe or boucharde, before being knocked away with the chisel. Granite tools must be held at an angle of 90 degrees to make any impact on the hard surface.

Safety precautions
Plastic goggles and respirators should always be worn when working with stone. Respirators protect the lungs from stone dust, some of which contains dangerous silicates.

Properly ventilated areas to work in are essential, and when power tools are being used and a lot of dust generated a special exhaust system to remove the dust is advisable.

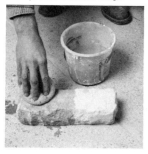
Stone-carving techniques Preparation 1. Tap the stone to test its soundness. An unflawed stone produces a clear 'ring'.

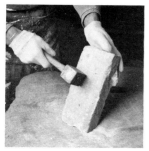
2. Wet the stone to gain an idea of its texture and what it will look like when polished.

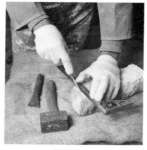
3. Before sawing, mark the cutting line with a serrated file. A hard stone should be marked with a wax pencil.

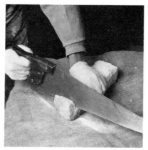
4. Saw the stone with short strokes. Hard stones may need special industrial equipment.

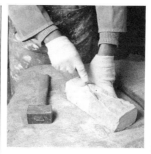
Roughing out 1. Mark the areas to be worked away with a serrated scalpel or, for more precise outlines, a wax pencil.

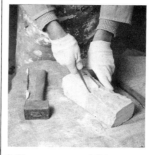
2. Measure any exact distances with dividers.

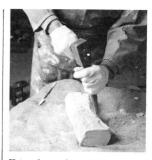
Using the pitcher 1. Cut away unwanted stone with the pitcher and a stonemason's hammer. Work along the edge.

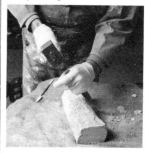
2. To vary the amount of stone which is cut away, change the angle of the pitcher.

19

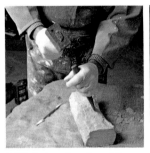

3. Work along the edges of the stone to create the broad outlines of the final carving.

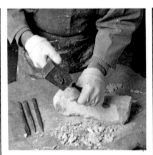

Using the claw 1. Work over the surface in one direction with the claw.

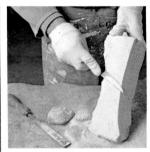

2. Next use the double files which come in several shapes and textures. Start with the coarse file and then use the finer ones.

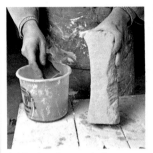

4. Wet the silicon carbide paper in the bucket, rub it on to the stone using a circular scouring motion.

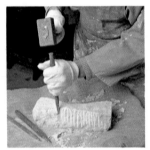

Using the point 1. More exact shaping begins with the point. Hit the point with the hammer at about 90°.

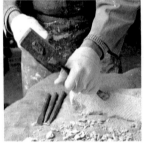

2. Work over the surface again from a different angle to create a criss-cross pattern, as with the point.

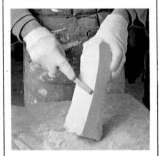

Finishing 1. Work over the surface with the file until it is completely smoothed.

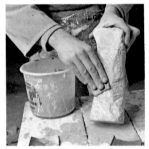

5. Repeat the process, working from coarse through to fine grades of the paper to give a very smooth surface.

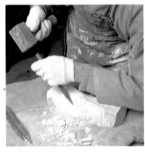

2. Having worked along in one direction, begin to smooth the surface by creating a criss-cross pattern.

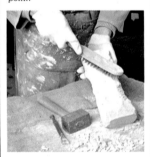

Brushing At intervals during the carving, brush away dust with a wire or hard bristle brush. Use a soft brush in later stages.

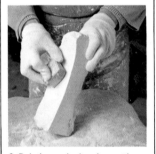

2. Rub the worked surface with carborundum stone. Rub to a perfectly even surface. If the stone is hard, use the carborundum wet.

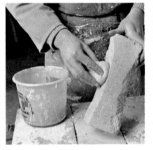

6. Give the stone a final sponge down to remove dust or particles of stone.

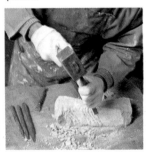

Using the flat The flat chisel is used to create a flatter surface and smoother finish. Work along the surface as before.

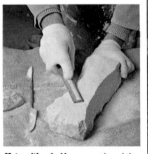

Using files 1. Having outlined the shape, go over the surface with a coarse stone file. Use the curved edge for rougher work.

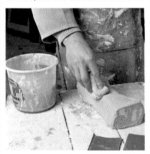

3. Wet the stone completely by squeezing water from a sponge.

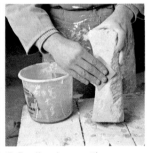

7. Finally rub over with emery cloth. When the stone is dry, buff with a soft, dry cloth to bring up the shine.

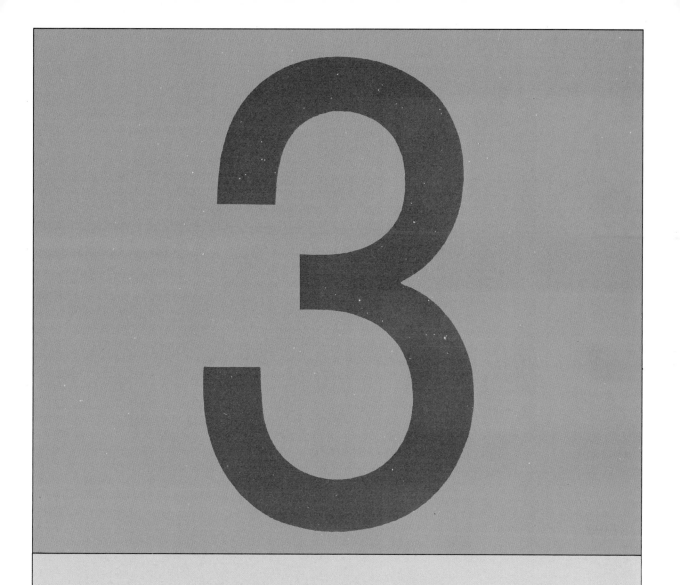

Carving wood.

History. Types of wood. Tools and equipment: Carving, Shaping, Carpentry, Tool sets, Fixing, Sharpening. **Techniques:** Drawing, Sawing, Gouging, Carving in the round, Finishing.

Wood-carving History

Wood is the oldest medium known to man. The craft of carving wood has been practised since the earliest times from the decoration of crude weapons and utensils to modern shapes and forms created by present-day sculptors.

The primitive craftsmen of Africa, Australasia, Mexico and Polynesia carved charms and masks for rituals which remained unchanged for centuries.

In ancient Egypt, too, carving held a ritualistic role and wood was used for effigies and tomb statues, as well as being used ornamentally on furniture and friezes. The Greeks were using carved wood inlaid with ivory and gold from about 800 BC, and Roman craftsmen decorated their furniture, boats and chariots with elaborate carvings.

In the eleventh century, wood-carving appeared in northern Europe, starting in Germany and spreading to the Low Countries and Britain. The European Gothic style emerged in the early twelfth century and flourished under wealthy church and private patronage into the early 1500s.

Artists and craftsmen were working in Italy at this time in the classical tradition now known as the Italian Renaissance. The impact of the fine carved interiors and furniture of the Renaissance spread rapidly across Europe, particularly influencing carvers in Flanders, and eventually England.

The prolific wood-carver Grinling Gibbons (1648–1721), working in England with such architects as Sir Christopher Wren (1632–1723), had a far-reaching effect because of his position as Master Carver to the Crown. His distinctive' and elegant work gained an international reputation and Gibbons's carvings can be seen in many homes and churches throughout Britain.

Wood-carvers today have moved away from their traditional place alongside architects and cabinet-makers. The severity of twentieth-century design has to some extent changed their role. Wood-carving nowadays flourishes as one of the fine arts, and the free-standing works of such fine sculptors as Henry Moore (born 1898) and Barbara Hepworth (1903–1975) enhance our environment today.

Wood-carving Types of wood

When choosing timber for carving, the colour and grain must be suitable for the work in hand. Fairly straight-grained woods, being not too difficult to work, are better choices for the beginner.

The sapwood, the new outside growth of the tree, is paler and wetter than the heartwood which is the mature, inner wood better suited to carving. The sapwood is removed before carving begins, as it tends to split easily. All timbers vary in moisture content and must be seasoned before use to avoid shrinkage and distortion. Woods also vary greatly in texture: oak, for example, is coarse textured while others, such as cherry and lime, have fine, even textures. It is worth noting that some woods give a good, polished finish, but others produce one which is poor and dull.

The softwoods, which include pine and cedar, are readily available and come in large sizes. The wood has a tendency to split and it is advisable to use the slow-growing varieties. Yellow pine is particularly good for carving larger works, but Parana pine should be avoided.

Of the many hardwoods some two dozen are popularly used for carving. Oak, mahogany and walnut are traditional favourites; lime or basswood, sometimes called 'the sculptor's wood', is very easy to work, as are the fruitwoods; cherry is particularly favoured for its rich colour. Very hard woods such as ebony and

lignum-vitae are only suitable for small works.

Alder This is a soft, easily workable wood. It is usually reddish with an indistinct grain.

Apple This is a hard, easily workable wood. It is red in colour with an indistinct grain.

Beech Beech is easy to work; and it is not difficult to obtain a good finish. Beech is light brown in colour with a close, and rather uninteresting grain.

Boxwood Boxwood is a very hard, dense wood most suited to small work. It is pale yellow with an indistinct grain. It gives a good finish.

Cedar This close-grained, easily workable softwood varies in colour from yellow through red to brown.

Chestnut This is a moderately hard wood with a tendency to split. It is light brown in colour with a distinct grain. Chestnut is durable, and gives a good finish.

Ebony Ebony is a very hard wood which is difficult to obtain and to work and suitable for small pieces. It varies from dark brown to black and has a distinct fine grain. It takes a good finish.

Elm This hard wood is sometimes difficult to work but it finishes well. In appearance, it is yellow to reddish-brown with a marked grain.

Holly Holly is an easily workable hard wood which is smooth, white and has a fine grain.

Lime Lime—called basswood in the USA—is a fairly

soft, very easily workable wood. It is pale yellow with few grain markings. It is also readily obtainable.

Mahogany This is a rather hard wood, usually easy to work. It has a reddish-brown colour with a variable grain.

Maple This close-grained, medium hard wood finishes well. Its colour varies from light to reddish-brown.

Oak Many varieties of oak exist but it is generally a hard wood which is fairly easy to work. The wood is very durable, and takes a good finish but continues to check—or crack—for some time. Its appearance varies from yellow to dark brown and it has a distinctive grain.

Pear Pear is a moderately hard, even-textured wood which is fairly easy to work. It is light reddish-brown in colour with a close grain. Fruit woods such as pear, apple, holly and plum are only available in relatively small pieces.

Pine This soft wood is easy to work, depending on the variety, but it is prone to splitting and to woodworm, and so is not very suitable for carving. Its colour varies from pale yellow to dark orange with a strongly marked grain.

Plum This hard wood is usually fairly easy to work. It is pinkish in colour with a distinct grain.

Rosewood Rosewood is a hard wood which is not easy to obtain or to work. However, sculptors value it for its even texture and colouring which varies through reddish-brown, purple and black.

Sandalwood This is a hard, scented wood which is usually used for small, detailed work. It is yellowish-brown in colour.

Satinwood Satinwood is a hard wood which can be difficult to work because it splits easily. In colour it is light orange with a patterned grain.

Sycamore This moderately hard wood, which is sometimes difficult to work, is white in colour. It is obtainable in large sizes.

Teak Teak is a hard wood, which is moderately easy to work. It is yellowish-brown with a distinctive grain.

Walnut Walnut is a hard, easily worked wood with a good finish, although it is expensive and difficult to obtain. It is chocolate brown in colour with a richly marked grain.

Yew This is a hard, durable wood with a good finish, which is easy to obtain. In appearance it varies from creamy to reddish-brown, with a distinctive grain.

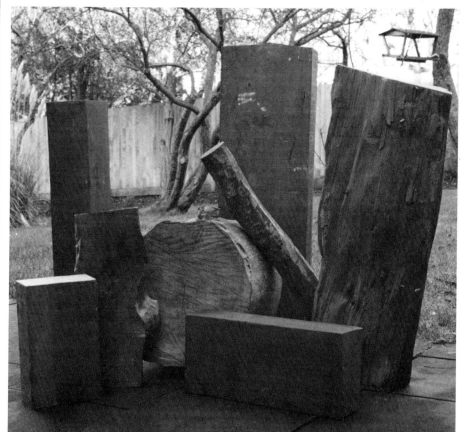

Types of wood
Colour and grain are important factors in determining the sculptor's choice of wood. These woods are reasonably readily available and suitable for carving: from **left** to **right:** pitch pine, oak, yew, elm, mahogany, apple, teak and cedar. Wood for carving comes in different shapes and states. For example, the apple is just a trunk with the bark removed, the elm is in the form of a 'cheese', a cross-section of the trunk, the cedar has been quartered and the pitch pine, mahogany and teak are planks. Each wood has particular characteristics which the prospective sculptor should be aware of. For example, the fruit woods like apple, pear and plum are only available in fairly small pieces — determined by the size of the trunk. Many tropical woods such as ebony and mahogany are becoming increasingly expensive and difficult to obtain.

Wood-carving Tools and equipment

T he wood-carver's tools fall into three main groups: carving tools, shaping tools and carpentry tools. A selection of the three types is needed by any prospective carver.

Carving
The gouge and the chisel are essential items. The gouge has a curved cutting edge which ranges from a narrow U-shape to just a slight curve. Both the chisel and gouge come in various shapes including bent and curved, enabling inaccessible hollows to be carved. V-shaped gouges are known as veiners and fluters and are used for fine work.

Shaping
Rasps, files, and rifflers are the basic wood shapers. A file is finer than a rasp; a riffler has a curved edge for rounded shapes. The Surform shaper has a built-in space for shavings to prevent clogging.

Carpentry
Of the many saws the half-rip saw which cuts both with and across the grain of the wood is the most useful. The bow saw is used for cutting curves and the fret saw for flat pieces. A wooden mallet is another essential tool and it is important to select one that is not too heavy and tiring to hold.

Tool sets
It is not necessary to buy a comprehensive set of carving tools at first. Beginners' sets with six or nine basic tools are available and can be supplemented later.

Although carving tools are frequently sold without handles, it is more convenient to buy them with handles already fitted. Handles are usually smooth or fluted, the latter being better for gripping.

When not in use, tools should be kept in a soft case to protect the cutting edges. Cases can either be bought or made from strong canvas.

Fixing
The bench on which to fix the work should be very firm and ideally have a top of at least 2in (5cm) thick—a reinforced kitchen table makes an adequate substitute. For free-standing work a carver's stand is more convenient than a bench as it enables the carver to move around the work more easily.

There are several ways of fixing the work in position. A carver's vice may be screwed to the top of the bench and is more suitable than the carpentry vice, which is fitted to the edge. A carpenter's vice often suffices, however, for smaller pieces. A bench screw, which bolts the work to the bench through a hole in the work surface, can be used for free-standing pieces, while for flatter work G-clamps are useful.

Sharpening
All new tools need to be sharpened and, although sharpening is not difficult, very worn or damaged tools must first be reground by an expert. Hard woods tend to blunt tools very quickly.

Oilstones and slipstones, varying in degree of coarseness, are used for sharpening. The shape of the tool must be retained and the correctly shaped slipstone should be used for each tool. The final sharpening is done with a fine stone such as Washita.

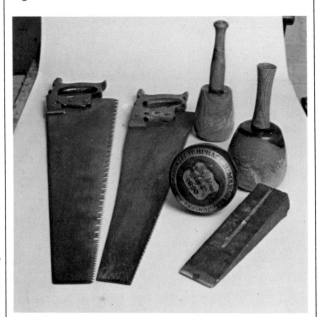

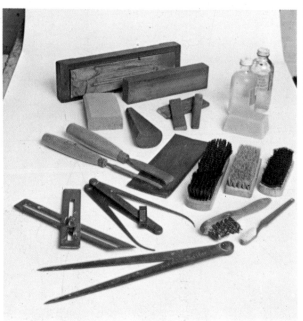

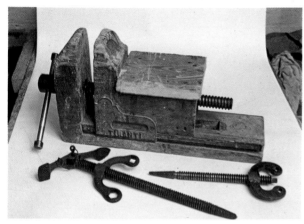

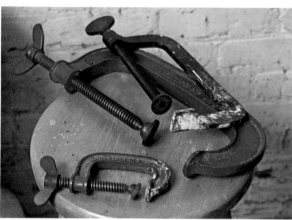

Gouges (bottom) A selection of gouges are necessary for any wood-carving. This selection shows (from **left** to **right**) flat gouges, U-shaped gouges, veiner, back-bent gouges. The size and type of gouge should be suited to the stage of the work, the size of the piece of wood and the effect you wish to achieve.

Rasps and rifflers (below)
There is a wide range of rasps and rifflers available for the sculptor to choose from. The rasps come in different degrees of coarseness. The rifflers are available in a wide variety of sizes and shapes which include pointed, flat, spoon-shaped and rounded.

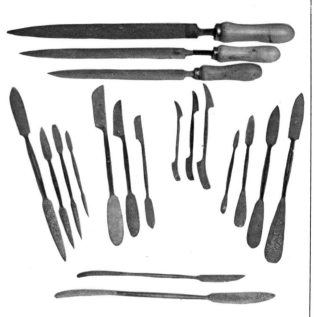

Wood-carving tools and equipment Wood-carving requires a number of different tools for the various processes involved in producing a carving. There is a very wide range available; the beginner would need a basic selection only. Saws (fine and large toothed), mallets and a boaster (**above left**) are used to begin shaping the wood. Mallets are used with the gouges. The mallet should be the correct size for the size of the gouge and the piece of wood. When working the wood, it is important to ensure that the wood is held firmly, for example, in the wood vice or by clamps (**top**). G-clamps (**above**) can be used to hold pieces of wood together or to hold them to the bench. Equipment for finishing (**left**) includes oilstones and carborundum stone (**top left**), linseed oil and real turpentine (**top right**). Brushes (**centre right**) and a soft cloth are also used for polishing. The leather strop (**centre**) is used for sharpening the tools, while the callipers, dividers and adjustable set-square (**bottom**) are used for measuring the wood.

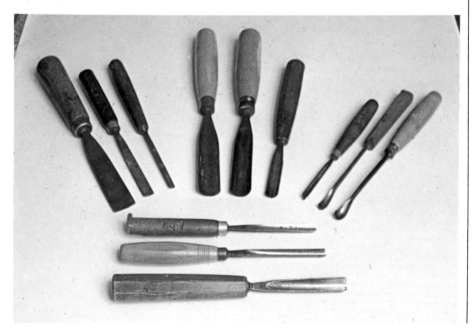

25

Wood-carving Techniques

A good carver makes use of the special qualities of wood; natural contours, the direction of the grain and the colour variations are each used to advantage because wood, more than almost any other medium, imposes its natural qualities upon the finished product. Carving is nevertheless a craft, and certain basic techniques must be mastered.

Drawing or marking out

It is often helpful to make preliminary sketches before starting work, particularly with more formal carving when it will also be necessary to transfer the drawings on to the wood. This is usually done by taping the full-size drawing on to the wood with carbon paper underneath and then tracing the outline, or, alternatively, by cutting a template and drawing round it.

Sawing

Initially, the surplus wood is removed with a saw. A bow saw can be used for curved surfaces, but care must be taken at this stage to leave plenty of room for finer carving. Difficult or undulating surfaces can be removed by making a number of saw cuts across the grain up to the required outline, and then carving away the remainder with a chisel or gouge.

Gouging

In the early stages of a work, the boasting in, the gouge is used with a mallet. The gouge should be as large as comfort and the size of the piece of wood allows and should be used across the grain of the wood in order not to lift the wood along the fibre. For the later, finer stages the mallet is not needed as hand-pressure on the gouge is sufficient.

When gouging, it is important to note the grain. If a deep U-shaped gouge is being used it must be remembered that two directions of grain are being carved and one or other will often produce a torn finish. This can sometimes be remedied, however, by using a sharper tool or by changing direction.

Carving in the round

Three-dimensional carving known as 'in the round' demands easy access. The wood should be firmly fixed at a convenient working angle and, ideally, there should be sufficient room to view the work from all directions. Time should be taken 'reading' the wood, noticing its special points, and planning the work.

If drawings are used, they should be full-size elevations of the sides plus one other elevation—probably the top, or plan. It is advisable to remove the waste wood from the side elevations first. After this rough shaping comes the boasting in, or rounding, then the more detailed modelling, and finally the finishing.

Finish

The chief reason for a finish, or protective coating, is to preserve the wood. Light coloured wood is especially prone to discolouration and shows fingerprints and grease stains. A finish also minimizes the effects of a dry or damp atmosphere.

Wax polish, a traditional finish, can be made by melting lumps of beeswax with an equal quantity of real turpentine and some linseed oil which helps add lustre to the wood. The mixture is applied cold, left for a few minutes, and then polished. Wax polish can also be used over a thin coat of polyurethane varnish which has been glass-papered to dull the gloss, or over a coat of linseed oil which has been allowed to dry. Outdoor sculptures should be sealed against heat and rain with several thin coats of sealing and rubbed down with fine glass-paper when completely dry.

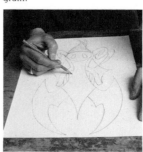

Wood-carving techniques 1. Examine the piece of wood to note any particular features such as the grain.

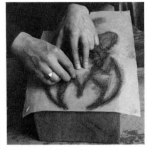

4. Draw over the outline with graphite or pencil on the back of the tracing paper.

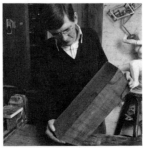

2. Draw a preliminary sketch of the proposed carving. It is best to draw the plan — or top — view first.

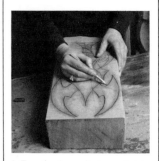

5. Transfer the preliminary sketch on to the wood from the tracing paper.

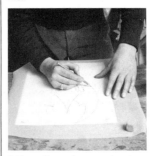

3. Trace the preliminary sketch on to tracing paper.

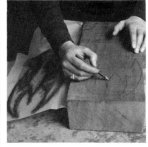

6. If necessary, reinforce the sketch directly on the wood using charcoal, Chinagraph or pencil.

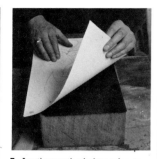

7. Another method of transferring the sketch is to place a sheet of carbon paper on the wood under the sketch.

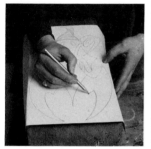

8. Transfer the sketch on to the wood by going over it on top of the carbon paper.

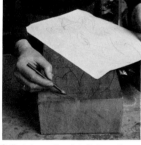

9. Reinforce the sketch directly on the wood.

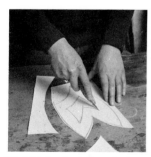

10. A third method of transferring the sketch is to use a template. Draw out the design and cut it out with scissors or a scalpel.

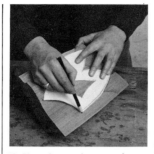

11. Place the template on to the wood, bend to shape. Remember that you are working from two to three dimensions.

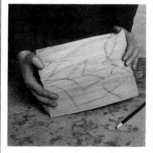

12. When the outline sketch is completed, carving can begin. The initial idea will develop during the carving process.

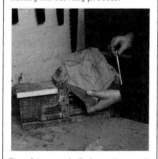

Roughing out 1. To keep the wood steady during carving, place in a wood vice and wedge if necessary.

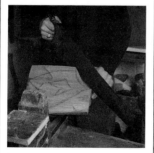

2. Saw off any excess wood reasonably close to the drawn outline.

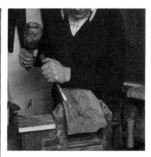

3. Use a medium-sized round gouge to begin working towards the final shape.

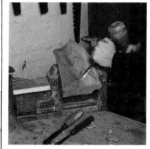

4. The round gouge is used to create a reasonably smooth and even surface.

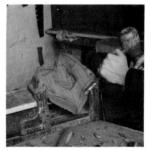

5. The roughing out process should continue until the piece of wood approximates to the proposed final shape.

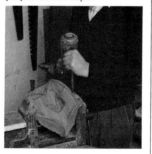

6. Select the size of gouge which is suited to the size of the wood. Move the wood round as you work.

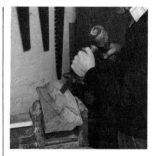

7. Work down to the drawn outline using a smaller flat gouge to smooth the surface further.

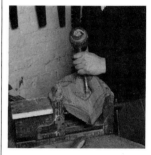

8. Mark out the central area using a flattish gouge. Keep well within the drawn outline.

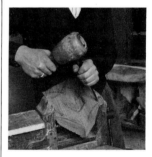

9. Hollow out the central area with a small flattish gouge. Do not carve too close to the outlines.

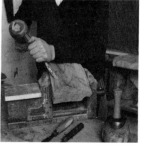

10. Shape across the grain of the wood to avoid lifting the wood fibres along the grain.

27

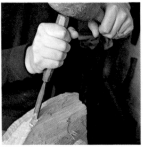

Using the gouge 1. If the gouge penetrates the wood too deeply, as in this picture, it will lift too much wood.

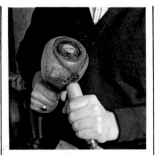

Using the mallet 1. Make contact with the handle of the gouge at about 90°. With a small gouge use a small mallet.

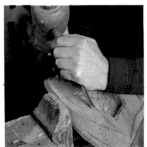

Using the veiner 1. The veiner, a V-shaped gouge, is useful for working in tight or small corners.

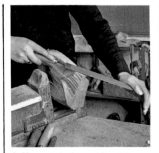

2. Use mainly the middle of the rasp for more pressure. Start working with a coarse rasp and then use a finer one.

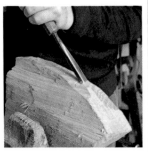

2. To use the gouge correctly hold at an angle of about 45°. The angle varies with the size of the gouge and the wood.

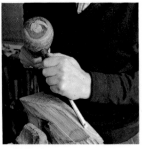

2. With a large gouge use a larger mallet. The weight of the mallet stroke depends on the wood, tool and stage of the work.

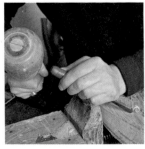

2. It is also used for cutting a deep groove, for example, to create surface patterns.

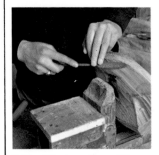

3. The riffler is smaller and finer than the rasp and gives added smoothness to the surface.

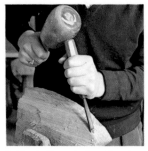

3. Gradually work along the edges of the wood to smooth it out. As in the roughing out, work over the whole surface area.

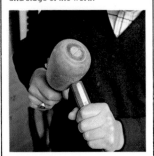

Using the flat gouge 1. To flatten out the surface use a flat gouge and a mallet. Work along the edges.

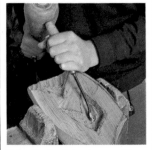

Using the back-bent gouge This gouge is used for digging out wood. Back-bent gouges come in different sizes.

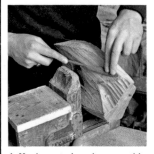

4. Use long strokes where possible and steady the end of the riffler with one or two fingers.

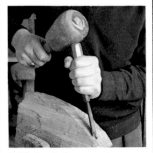

4. Work with the gouge down to within about ¼ in of the desired final surface.

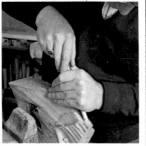

2. Then work along the surfaces again guiding the gouge by hand. This gives you more control.

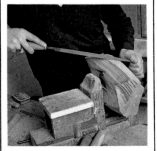

Using rasps and rifflers 1. The rasp is used for smoothing the surface. Bring the rasp across and with the grain.

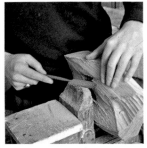

5. After a few strokes with the riffler, feel the wood to test the degree of smoothness and feel where to use the tool next.

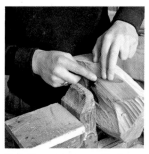

6. As the surface is smoothed, use progressively finer rifflers. Some have spoon shaped ends for working curved shapes.

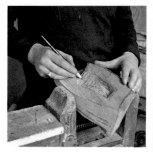

7. Next examine the wood and mark out the final shape more exactly. Use a Chinagraph or similar pencil which will not erase.

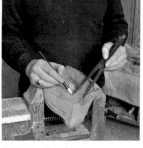

8. Use dividers for any exact measurements such as parallel lines.

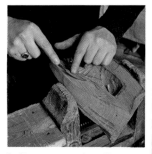

9. Alternate using the rifflers with examining the wood and, if necessary, further marking out.

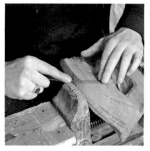

10. Use the rifflers until the surface is smooth enough to begin finishing.

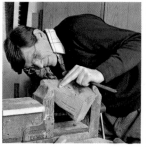

11. While working with the rifflers it is important to keep feeling and looking at the wood.

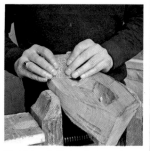

Finishing 1. To finish the surface first use a drawplate which has a bevelled cutting edge. Hold the plate at about 45°.

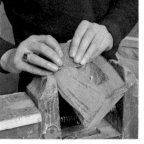

2. Draw the plate towards you. It cuts a thin layer of wood, clears out the pores of the wood and brings up the grain.

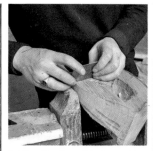

3. Move the drawplate forward to compress the surface fibres. This brings out the wood's gloss.

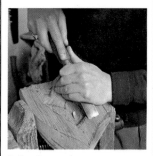

4. Finishing with a gouge creates a lively, textured surface. Use a wide flattish gouge. The bevel of the gouge burnishes the wood.

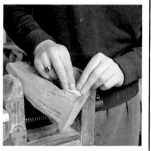

5. For a very smooth finish, use a craft knife blade. Hold at 60°. These blades are very sharp, so use with great care.

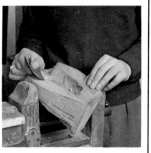

6. To continue smoothing the surface, use silicon carbide or sandpaper. Keep checking the smoothness of the finish.

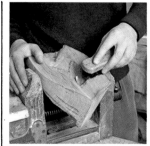

7. Using sandpaper fills the pores of the wood with dust. Brushing the dust away brings up the grain again.

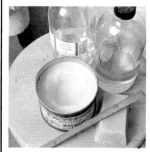

Polishing 1. You can use a good proprietary wax polish, but many carvers make their own from real turps, linseed oil and beeswax.

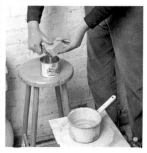

2. To make polish, first scrape or cut the wax into the tin. Small pieces melt more quickly.

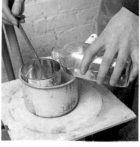

3. Place in a double boiler, melt the wax, add purefied linseed oil. Stir thoroughly to combine the wax and oil.

29

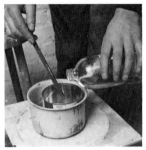

4. Add the real turpentine with great care as it is very inflammable.

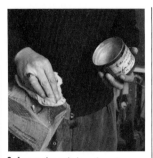

8. Leave the polish on for a few minutes while the turpentine evaporates.

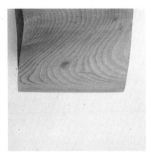

This piece of cedar has been finished until the surface is extremely smooth; however, it has not yet been polished.

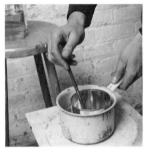

5. Stir the mixture until it is thoroughly mixed. This will take a few minutes.

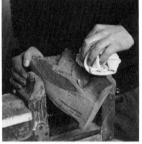

9. Buff up the surface with a soft cloth.

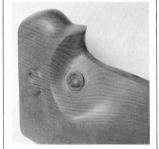

The surface of this sculpture in cedar has been polished to bring up a good shine and bring out the grain.

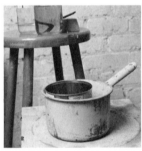

6. Allow the polish to set before using. It will be a pale yellow colour.

Finished woods
This piece of sycamore has been finished with a gouge. Note the textured surface.

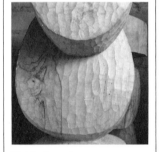

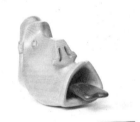

The completed sculpture by Rudy Leenders entitled *Demagogus vulgarus* combines polished cedar and polished teak.

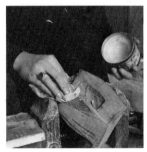

7. Apply polish to the wood surface with a soft cloth. Wax polish brings up the grain and adds a shine.

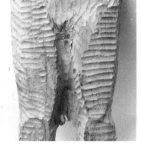

This piece of yew is being worked on with a U-shaped gouge. This gives the wood a ridged surface texture.

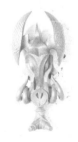

This other Leenders sculpture entitled *Caper politicus* is made of polished teak. Note the varied texture of the surface.

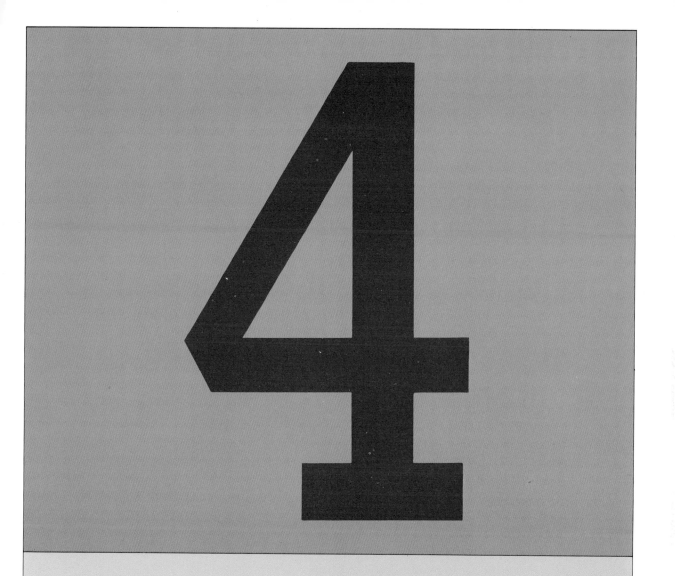

Carving foamed plastics.

History. Types of foam: Polystyrene, Polyurethane.
Tools and techniques: Joining and glueing, Colouring,
Heated tools.

Carving foamed plastics History

Foamed plastics are a comparatively new medium for the artist. Those already established, such as polystyrene and polyurethane, are being explored with enthusiasm by sculptors and designers both for their physical properties and for their ready availability.

Although polystyrene only came on to the market in 1938 and foamed polyurethane is an even more recent development, the use of these foams is already growing in popularity.

Painter and sculptor Jean Dubuffet (born 1901) was one of the first to use carved polystyrene, and many of the monumental works created by the French sculptor, Louis. Chavignier (born 1922), are made of foamed polyurethane.

Foamed plastics are also used extensively as large-scale carved moulds for cement and concrete sculptures, and as a light core for heavier substances.

Carving foamed plastics Types of foam

Foams are plastics which have been expanded with gas during their manufacture. They can be hard or soft, rigid or flexible. The two most practical and popular for carving are rigid polystyrene and rigid polyurethane, being strong, light and reasonably inexpensive.

Polystyrene
Being one of the thermoplastics group, polystyrene melts when heated and dissolves in certain solvents. It is non-toxic, but strong fumes are given off when polystyrene foam is heated. Good ventilation is essential, therefore, when heated tools are used. Polysty-

rene is highly flammable unless specially treated.

Expanded polystyrene, which is the type used for packaging, has a rather crumbly, open-cell texture. However, a denser material, the closed-cell, foamed polystyrene, known commercially as Styrofoam, is also available.

Polyurethane
It is a rigid, closed-cell material which varies in density. Polyurethane is a thermosetting resin so, unlike the polystyrenes, does not melt. It releases toxic fumes when exposed to heat and must therefore not be worked with heated tools.

Tools and types of foam
Foam is available is the form of either sheets (**3**) or blocks (**4**). Tools for cutting the material include a craft knife (**5**), knife (**6**) and scalpel (**7**). The hand-held hot wire cutter (**8**) can make very smooth cuts through the foamed plastic. The saw (**10**) is used for cutting off larger pieces of material. Pieces of foamed plastic can be glued together using PVA adhesive (**1**). The sculpture can be coated with plaster (**2**), which makes the surface more durable and means that you can use types of paint which would otherwise damage the actual polystyrene. It is possible, however, to use acrylic paints (**9**) directly on the polystyrene surface. Paint should be applied with standard paint brushes (**11**).

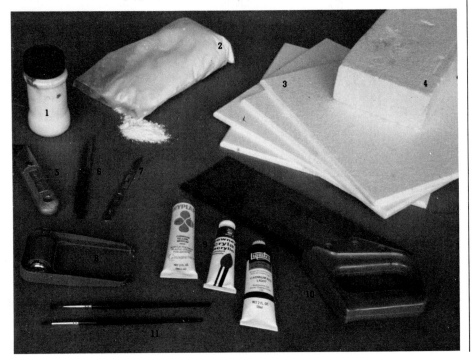

Carving foamed plastics Techniques

Most foams can be worked easily with standard wood-carving tools. The gouge and the chisel are best used with hand pressure only. Rasps, files, rifflers, planes and wire brushes are all suitable for shaping foam. Large blocks can be cut with a general purpose saw, while finer cutting is done with sharp knives and safety razor blades.

Joining and glueing

Of the several suitable adhesives for both polystyrene and polyurethane, a non-solvent glue such as PVA is used for polystyrene, and for polyurethane the rubber contact types are used.

Polystyrene can also be joined by applying solvent to the parts to be joined and holding them together, or by drawing a hot wire between two surfaces which are pressed together.

Colouring

As polystyrene is soluble in some substances, paints which contain such solvents must be avoided, unless the surface of the polystyrene is first coated with a thin layer of plaster of Paris. These include oils and polyester resins, and anything containing acetone or turpentine. Safe colourings for polystyrene include vinyl and acrylic paints.

As polyurethane is insoluble, it is unaffected by such reactions and the choice of paints and colourings is therefore very wide.

Heated tools

Although heated tools are ideal for cutting and carving polystyrene, they should not be used for polyurethane.

Hot wire cutters work on the principle of an electric current passing through a wire which softens and cuts the material. The wire should be of nickel chrome. A table model can be used for cutting large or simple shapes, while for modelling and cutting smaller surfaces a hand-cutter is useful.

An electric soldering iron or kitchen knife makes an ideal carving tool. Soldering irons can be bought with wire accessories of various shapes.

Detailed work is often done with needles or fine metal tools embedded in cork and heated over a flame.

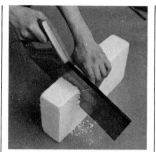

Cutting polystyrene 1. Blocks of polystyrene can be cut with an ordinary saw in the same way as a block of wood.

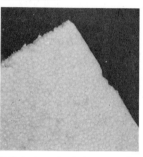

2. Cut edges of polystyrene can be rough and flaky owing to the composition of the material. The cutting edge should not drag.

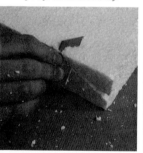

3. A sharp knife blade or safety razor blade is used to carve away small areas from the edges of the block.

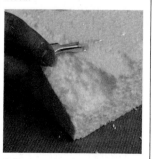

4. For extra detail small slivers of polystyrene can be removed with a sharp scalpel. The scalpel cuts are short and smooth.

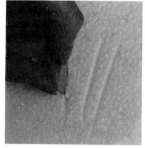

5. Knives can also be used to form pattern areas on flat surfaces by chipping into the block in various ways to create a texture.

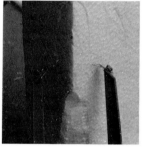

6. A hand-held hot wire tool will cut away pieces from a block. Hold the tool steady and do not force it through the material.

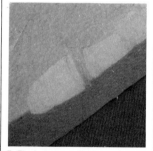

7. The hot wire melts the surface of the material and forms a smooth cut. Large cuts can be made with a table model of hot wire cutter.

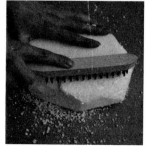

8. A wire brush roughens the surface of the polystyrene and erodes it gradually to make curved shapes and gentle angles.

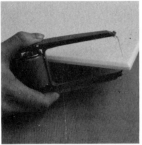

Cutting polystyrene with a hot wire 1. Hold the tool firmly and press the wire against one edge. Cut through gradually.

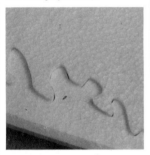

2. The heat in the wire dictates the speed with which it cuts. Do not force it. When the cut is finished, ease the pieces apart carefully.

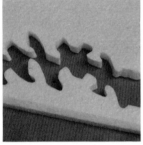

3. The hot wire cutter gives a very clean cut through the material and can be used for quite complicated shapes cut in any direction.

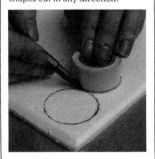

4. To cut a specific shape out of polystyrene, mark out the shape with a felt tip pen. Press lightly or it will dig into the material.

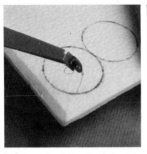

5. Cut out the shape carefully with the hot wire cutter, working just inside the marks so that they are not visible on the final object.

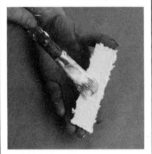

Glueing and joining 1. Coat the surfaces which are to be glued together with PVA adhesive, or other non-solvent glue.

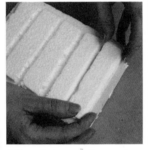

2. Press the pieces to be joined firmly together, and allow the glue to dry. In this case, relief shapes are being added to a block.

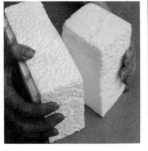

3. Two blocks of polystyrene can be joined in the same way. Press the glued sides together and leave them until the glue has dried.

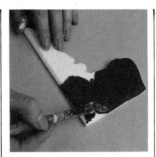

Making a painted relief 1. Cut the sections of the relief out of sheets or thin blocks and paint as required with acrylic colour.

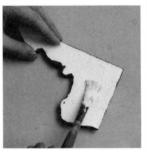

2. When the paint has dried, coat the underside of the pieces with an even layer of PVA adhesive.

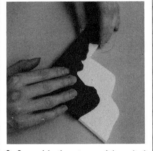

3. Assemble the pieces of the relief as required, pressing the glued surfaces firmly down. Leave them to dry.

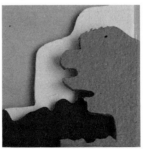

4. A relief can be built up of ready painted pieces, or may be assembled first and painted as a whole afterwards.

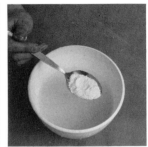

Coating with plaster 1. Mix plaster of Paris with water in a bowl until it has a thick, creamy consistency.

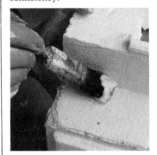

2. Pour plaster over the sculpture and use a brush to spread it into cracks and joints, until there is a thin, smooth layer all over.

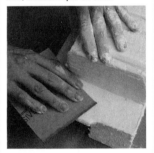

3. When the plaster has dried, any unevenness in the surface can be lightly rubbed with sandpaper to achieve a satisfactory surface.

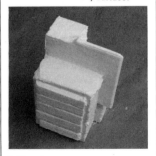

4. The plaster of Paris makes the sculpture more durable and the surface will now take paint.

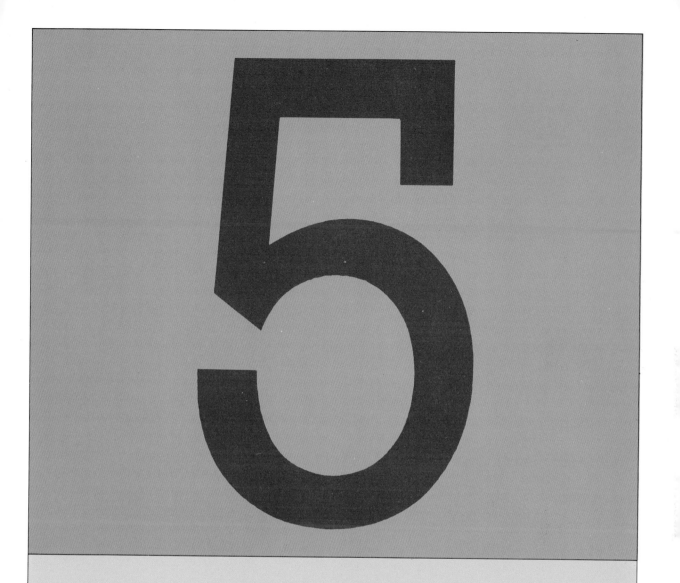

Modelling.

History. Armatures. Materials and techniques: Clay, Terracotta, Wax, Plaster, Glass fibre reinforced plastic. **Tools and equipment.**

Modelling History

Wax has been used as a modelling material for thousands of years. As it is soft and malleable, it is generally cast into a more permanent material such as bronze. Given adequate protection however, wax is reasonably durable itself, and indeed examples of wax modelling have been found in Egyptian tombs. In China, wax was used to produce ceremonial bronze vessels during the Shang dynasty (c.1766–c.1123 BC).

The ancient Greeks used wax not only for casting but to make toy dolls and religious figurines. The Romans made wax death masks of important personages.

Clay is probably the most commonly used modelling material as it is found throughout the world and indeed many examples of its use by ancient civilizations have survived. Terracotta works provide the earliest examples of man's use of clay as, in its simplest form, it is clay baked in a fire to render the shape permanent. The addition of sands to give the clay a coarser body and the sifting of impurities later allowed potters and sculptors more scope. Terracotta was used by the Greeks, Romans and Etruscans and later became a popular medium with such Renaissance sculptors as Ghiberti (1378–1455) and Donatello (1386–1466).

Pre-Columbian cultures, notably the Zacatenco (2000 BC–AD 100), produced beautiful examples of terracotta work, especially at Tlatilco where many small figures have been found.

Since the early part of the twentieth century modelling has not played a major role in the development of sculpture, despite its use by such figures as Giacometti (1901–1966), Marini (born 1901), Matisse (1869–1954) and Moore (born 1898). Modelling is still mostly concerned with the interpretation of the visual world in a figurative way as in the works of sculptors identified with the Pop era such as Edward Keinholz (born 1927) and Claes Oldenburg (born 1929). The modelling tradition has been kept alive most recently by the works of Ivor Abrahams (born 1935), Robert Graham (born 1938) and Charles Simonds (born 1945).

Modelling Armatures

It is possible to construct an armature—a skeleton on to which 'flesh' is added—simply with clothes hangers or pieces of wood. The only requirement is that it must be strong enough to support the weight of the modelling material. If the work is to be fired the armature is removed first and so the design must allow for this. Depending on the model being produced, the support of a back iron may be necessary to keep it upright.

Lead piping is suitable for small sculptures, although pieces of wood sealed with shellac or French polish may need to be bound on, to prevent sagging.

Aluminium square section wire is commonly used for armatures nowadays as it holds its shape better than lead but is still easily manipulated. Pieces of wood wired to the frame may be necessary to bulk out the model, prevent sagging and provide a key.

If the armature is intended to support a work being executed in plaster, concrete, glass fibre reinforced plastic, or any other material used for direct modelling then a mild steel armature may be more suitable as it will remain a part of the finished piece and will not require external support. Depending on the size of the model it may be made from welded metal conduit or twisted coat hangers. If plaster is to be used directly on to a steel armature, the armature must be sealed with a metal primer or varnish to prevent rust discolo-ration on the finished work. Binding wire may be found useful wound around the frame to provide a key.

Wire netting and expanded metal can be used to give shape to large models. Either can be used in conjunction with a steel or wooden armature, or it can be used on its own.

As a wooden armature will absorb any moisture in the medium being used, causing cracking or distortion, always seal with shellac or an oil-based primer. Wooden armatures are less satisfactory than those of soft metal, as they cannot be bent or twisted, should an alteration be required.

Armatures can also be made from tin cans, bottles or any other inert material that gives a solid support without increasing the weight of material needed for the finished model.

Polystyrene makes an excellent core for large-volume sculptures as it has good compressive strength characteristics. It can be cut with a hot wire, old saw or craft knife and shaped with a surform or a cheese grater; proprietary adhesives can be used to fix blocks together. Polystyrene should not be used as a core for glass fibre reinforced plastics as the fumes given off during curing attack polystyrene even when a barrier agent has been employed. If hot wire is used to cut polystyrene adequate ventilation and gas-masks should be used as poisonous fumes are produced.

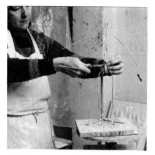

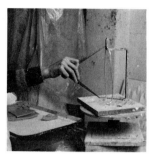

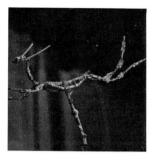

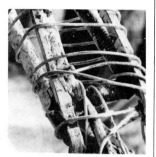

Making an armature 1. Bend the aluminium armature wire to the required shape. Support above the base board using a back iron.

2. Use pliers to wrap binding wire around. Knot the wire on each side and tighten up to hold the armature steady.

1. This wood and wire armature is for a model of a bounding hare. The basic shape and expression of movement are clearly visible.

2. Use wood bound with wire to shape the legs and head. Wind wire around 4 pieces of wood to give the body a box-like shape.

Modelling Tools and equipment

Wood craft shops supply modelling tools in all shapes and sizes. Clay tools are usually made of boxwood, but plastic ones are also available; steel modelling tools are best for plaster work.

Clay
Household items such as kitchen knives, wooden spoons, rolling-pins and penknives are just as effective as purpose-made tools. Broken hacksaw blades are invaluable for creating flat areas and for removing indentations by cross-scraping.

A baseboard made from thick ply sealed to prevent water absorption, plumbline, callipers, tape measure and plant spray complete the basic tool kit.

If working clay regularly a plaster bat (18 × 18 × 3in or 46 × 46 × 8cm) is useful. The clay is soaked until soft and then placed on the dry plaster surface which absorbs water. The clay is turned once or twice and wedged until the desired consistency is obtained.

Wax
Purpose-made plaster modelling tools, dental instruments, craft knives, scribers, nails or pencils are all suitable, and a glass or marble surface is required.

Plaster
A baseboard similar to that required for clay and Surform tools, which are designed not to clog with damp plaster, is particularly useful. Plaster modelling tools with a variety of shaped ends are suited to small works. Improvised tools include an old saw, cheese grater, axe and an old wood chisel.

Glass fibre reinforced plastics
Brushes are needed for impregnating rags with resin, and craft knives, scissors or spatulas are used for modelling. Rubber gloves and barrier creams are essential.

Tools for clay modelling The first essential is a baseboard (**6**) made of a good quality material, such as plywood. Modelling tools come in many different shapes and sizes. The best quality ones are made of boxwood (**7**), although plastic ones (**4**) may be suitable for beginners. Modelling tools are used for a variety of purposes from smoothing out a clay surface to creating texture in clay. Inside callipers (**9**) and outside callipers (**8**) are used for calculating interior and exterior measurements respectively. Other useful tools include a rolling pin (**1**), wooden spoons (**2**), a spray (**3**) for keeping the clay moist, kitchen knives (**10**), broken hacksaw blades (**11**), a penknife (**12**) and a plumbline (**5**).

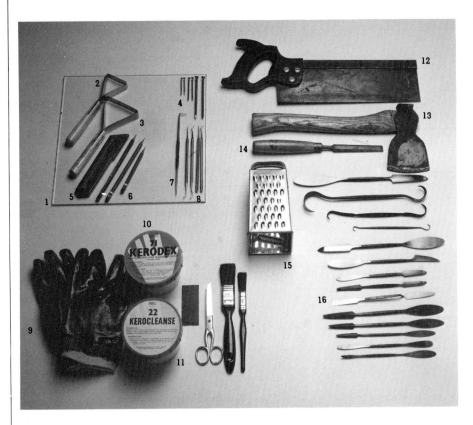

Modelling tools For working with different modelling substances, a variety of tools are needed. For wax modelling, the following are necessary: a glass (**1**) or marble surface, a wax scraper, either small (**2**) or large (**3**), a scriber (**7**), dental instruments for detail work (**8**), nails (**4**), a craft knife (**5**) and pencils (**6**). For modelling in glass fibre reinforced plastics, safety equipment, such as protective gloves (**9**), barrier cream (**10**), and cleansing cream (**11**), is vital. Also useful are scissors (**13**), brushes (**14**) and a spatula (**12**). For modelling in plaster, a range of modelling tools is (**16**) required. These tools come in a wide variety of sizes and shapes. The latter include, for example, flats, spoons, curves and rounds. Each tool has two ends which are different shapes and can be easily manipulated. When modelling, do not be afraid to improvise; many kitchen implements and household tools, such as a cheese grater (**15**), saw (**12**) and axe (**13**) and old wood chisel (**14**) have a place in the modeller's range of equipment.

Modelling Materials and techniques

Clay

Its popularity as a modelling material lies in its sensitivity to handling, particularly for fine detail. It can be used in a firm or soft state or combinations of hardness to produce the surface required. Different hardnesses of clay produce different handling qualities, indeed the French sculptor Rodin (1840–1917) kept clay in varying states of hardness for different stages of the modelling process.

Modelling is essentially an additive process, the shape required being blocked out and the surface form achieved by the addition of pellets of clay in such a way as to reveal the underlying structure. The basic form should be established from the start when blocking out and the clay applied to the entire sculpture, no one area being finalized too early. The viewpoint of the sculptor should be changed frequently both laterally and vertically.

A model that is being worked on should be kept moist by occasional spraying with a plant spray or by flicking a damp brush. Care should be taken not to soak the model as it may sag or lose detail.

If the model is left, even for a short time, it should be covered with a damp cloth and a plastic bag, such as a dustbin liner, used to make an airtight cover. If the model is very detailed or nearing completion, the damp cloth can be kept away from the surface by inserting matchsticks or nails at the high projection so that they protrude about one inch (2.5cm). Alternatively, a space frame can be constructed to fit over the model and support the cloth.

Terracotta

The advantage of using terracotta is that the finished model is the direct result of the sculptor's skill, no intermediary stage such as casting taking place.

When modelling with terracotta it is important to ensure that no air pockets or foreign bodies such as plaster are trapped in the clay or it may explode during firing. It is best to avoid attaching thin sections of clay to sections of greater volume, as drying out may cause cracks to appear between the two. This can be overcome by allowing the model, when almost complete, to dry until 'leather' hard; it can then be cut in half with a cheese wire or fine blade and hollowed out to reduce the amount of clay in the thick sections. The thickness of the walls of clay should be kept as even as possible .to reduce the likelihood of cracking and uneven drying. The edges of the two halves should then be roughened and slip (liquid clay) applied to one section before pressing the two sections firmly together.

Final cleaning up of the modelling is then carried out so that the joint will not be noticeable; a small puncture must be made into any hollowed-out sections to allow air to escape during firing.

If an armature has been used, the model has to be split to allow its removal. Small-scale standing figures can be produced, using only an external support.

A back iron is fitted with two prongs on to which a ball of clay is added to form the abdomen. A bed of clay is laid on the modelling board (which should first be sprinkled with sand or grog to prevent sticking) and two rolls of clay are then attached between the bed and the ball of clay to form the legs. A piece of clay flattened in the hand is attached to the top of the ball to form the back. Some loosely screwed-up paper is placed against this and a further piece of clay added to form the front. The paper will be burnt out during firing leaving a hollow trunk which, again, reduces the possibility of cracking. Clay is then added to form the head and arms, and as it gradually dries out the detailed modelling can be executed. Thus it is possible to produce a figure that does not require cutting or hollowing out.

Once it is self-supporting, but before it dries out completely, the model is withdrawn from the supporting prongs and the holes made good. Finally a hole is pierced through the navel to allow air to escape during the firing process.

A coarse grade clay is most suitable, especially for beginners modelling in terracotta, as it allows air to escape more easily and is more tolerant of varying thicknesses of section.

Firing should be carried out slowly even when the model has been allowed to dry out for a long period. If after firing the colour is raw and flat compared to its appearance in the unfired state, a coat of wax can be applied; this also helps to protect the porous surface from dirt. The model should be melted until it is just possible to handle and a small amount of wax melted in turpentine, using a double boiler, should be applied liberally to the model with a big, soft brush. This process can be repeated until the desired finish is achieved, giving a final rub with a soft cloth to remove excess wax.

Clay is best stored in a container such as a dustbin with a tight-fitting lid. A damp sack placed over the clay helps it to retain moisture, and if it dries out it can be soaked in a bin or basin until soft and then wedged to obtain an even consistency.

Wax

As it permits alterations and reshaping, wax is an excellent medium for small-scale modelling. Its sensitivity to pressure and detailed work make it superior to many more modern modelling compounds, but its delicate nature generally requires it to be cast into a more permanent material such as bronze.

The wax used for modelling is normally microcrystalline and is a synthetic product. Traditionally, beeswax was used which, with the addition of turpentine, tallow or rosins, could be made in various hardnesses giving different handling characteristics.

Working methods for wax vary from carving from a solid block to building up in a similar fashion to clay. If the form required is best made using sheets of wax, a block should be cut up and melted in a double boiler. It can then be poured out on to a cold, damp level surface such as glass or marble and allowed to solidify. (Sheets of wax may be stored and when needed placed in warm water to make them malleable enough to use—they will need to be dried before they will stick together.)

The shapes required may be produced by building dykes from clay or wood on the surface used and these must be damp too. The form can then be achieved by melting one edge of a shape, with a candle or warm blade, and pressing a second against it. A model can quickly be built up using coils and pellets as well as sheets of wax. Modelling tools warmed over a candle are used to work or cut the model and to shape it.

Plaster

Concrete, papier-mâché and plaster are all considered permanent forms of modelling since they do not need to be cast. Concrete can be built up on an armature of wire netting or glass fibre matting; it is not recommended as a modelling medium, however, since its properties preclude fine work and once set any filing destroys the surface. Papier-mâché is useful for large lightweight structures and is built up on an armature of wire with newspaper bound around it.

Having made a suitable armature, plaster models may require bulking out with paper or wire netting in order to reduce the amount of plaster necessary. Wads of newspaper should be tied to the armature with string, making sure that the padding remains below the final surface.

Scrim dipped in plaster is then wound round the armature and padding to form a jacket; two or three coats suffice for most work. It is advisable to use the scrim in short lengths for easy handling.

When the basic shape has been achieved the final

surface layer of plaster is applied, taking care to keep the model damp. If left even for a short time the model will require wetting; otherwise the hardened plaster will absorb water from the new mix, causing cracking and flaking. The final surface layer can be applied with the hands or any suitable tool, such as a trowel, knife or spatula, but the surface should be etched to provide a key for additional plaster to adhere to. A hacksaw blade or serrated knife is useful for this and also for tracing and removing unwanted indentations.

Should the setting process need to be retarded, a small quantity of glue-size solution is added to the water before the plaster is mixed in. This method provides a long period in which the plaster can be used, and the more glue size solution added the longer the period. It also strengthens the plaster. Alternatively the plaster-and-water mix can be left to stand for 10 minutes without stirring. Although this method provides a weaker plaster, it is useful when undercutting or when patching a broken sculpture.

If a plaster sculpture is to be mended, the pieces are first thoroughly soaked in water until all air bubbles have disappeared. New plaster may then be applied and the pieces held together until the plaster has set. Cellulose fillers—such as Unibond or Polyfilla—provide an easy alternative to this process, but because of the difference in hardness, care must be taken when sanding down.

Glass fibre reinforced plastic

Resins laminated with glass fibre are useful for direct modelling where speed, strength and lightness of weight are important, but they are not as responsive as clay or wax to detail.

The simplest method is to cover a basic armature of wire mesh, steel or wood with rags impregnated with lay-up resin. These can be bulked out with paper or drawn in by tying with string—rubber gloves should be used to avoid skin contact and the work surface covered with polythene. The manufacturer's instructions on the storage and handling of resins and catalysts should be heeded.

Once the rags impregnated with resin have hardened, usually within 30 minutes, the shape can be built up using glass fibre impregnated with lay-up resin to strengthen the form. The final surface is achieved by applying a coat of fibre tissue and gel-coat or thixotropic resin, possibly with a filler added to facilitate application by a spatula or knife.

The surface can be finished with old files or rasps or wet-and-dry carborundum paper. Files tend to clog frequently, but they can be cleaned in well-ventilated areas provided a gas-mask is worn by burning out the resin in a naked flame. Carborundum wheels fitted to an electric drill can also be used in well-ventilated areas provided a mask is used.

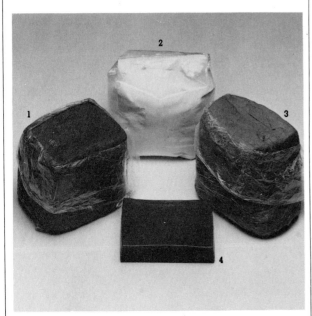

Modelling materials Models can be made of several main types of material. Terracotta (**1**) is modelled and then fired into a finished work. Plaster (**2**), clay (**3**) and wax (**4**) can all be cast into metal or resin, for example.

Modelling is either a finished process or the first stage of the longer and more complex casting process. Resin, a more recent development, is not as responsive as clay and wax, but is quick and light to work with.

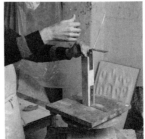

Modelling in clay 1. Make an aluminium wire armature. For an animal's head, use an angle bracket for support.

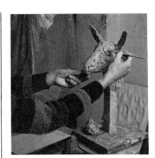

3. When the armature is covered in clay, begin to smooth it out with a modelling tool. In modelling, work from life or drawing .

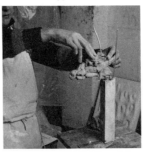

2. Begin to add the clay to the armature. Start between the ears. In modelling heads, the neck and head proportions are vital.

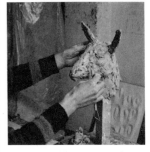

4. Begin to add in texture with a wire tool. This tool is also used for working up detail, such as the eyes.

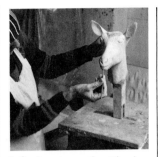

5. Continue to smooth out the clay and work up the detail gradually, until the model is complete.

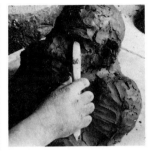

4. Use a tool to gouge out cavities and detail features. Work with hands and tools until the model is complete.

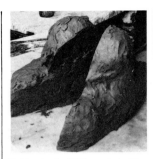

8. The clay is still damp, but will not sag with its own weight. Draw the halves of the model gently apart.

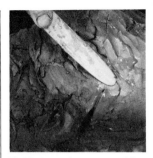

12. Work over the join around the whole model with fingers and modelling tools so that it is completely concealed.

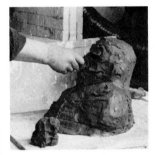

Terracotta modelling 1. Rough out the basis of the model in terracotta clay until the overall shape is apparent.

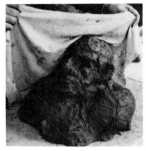

5. If the model is to be left overnight or for any length of time before further work is done, cover it with a damp cloth.

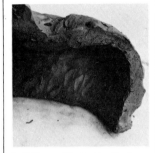

9. Hollow out the inside of both halves with modelling tools until all the clay is of the same depth. Smooth down with the fingers.

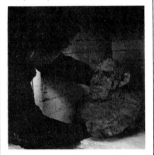

13. When the model is ready for firing, put it in the kiln. Heating to the required temperature makes the clay durable and hard.

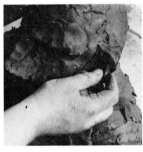

2. Add extra clay where needed and begin to form specific shapes and details, working the fresh clay to the basic shape.

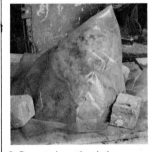

6. Cover it also with polythene, loosely draped over and weighted on all sides. The model will remain fresh and damp.

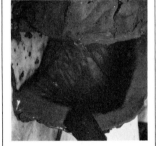

10. Paint thin clay slip around the edges of the hollowed out forms to soften the edges slightly and act as an adhesive.

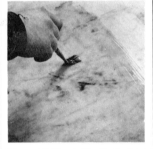

Wax modelling 1. The first task in wax modelling is to prepare a sheet of wax. Spread oil evenly over a marble slab.

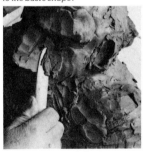

3. Use a spatulate modelling tool to remove surplus clay and carve out shapes. Continue smoothing out the shapes with the fingers.

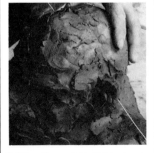

7. When the model is finished and has dried out a little (but is not completely dry), cut it in half by drawing wire through it.

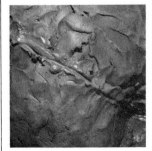

11. Press the two halves of the model together, so that they are perfectly joined. Some of the slip will ooze out from the join.

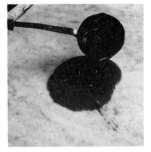

2. Heat the wax until it is liquid, and scoop some out with a ladle. Pour it quickly and evenly over the oiled marble surface.

41

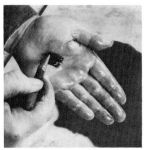

3. The wax must be allowed to cool slightly, but not too much. Meanwhile, brush oil over the palms of the hands.

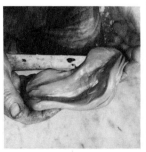

7. The wax is ready for modelling when it is in a pliable lump with a texture similar to soft toffee. If it hardens too much, it will crack.

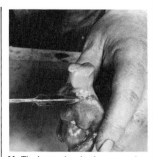

11. The hot tool melts the wax and gently moulds the forms together. First work up the basic shape of the form required.

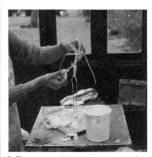

2. Twist some thinner wire around the armature to create a key so that the plaster will adhere to the wire.

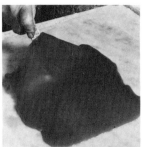

4. Lift the wax carefully with a broad, flat knife, so that it lifts as a whole skin from the marble without cracking.

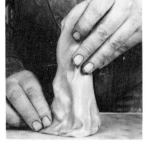

8. Start to model the wax into the basic shape required, and continue the modelling process with hands and tools.

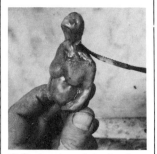

12. Continue to work, heating the tool again when necessary, and begin to describe details of form and surface finish.

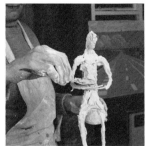

3. Dip scrim or bandage into the plaster and wrap it round the armature. This builds up the core of the model. Allow to set.

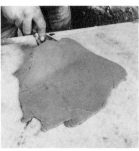

5. Flip the wax over with the knife so that the other side cools flatly against the slab. It should still be warm and flexible.

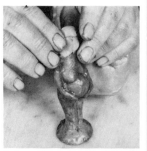

9. A correction or repair can be made, to a wax model with fresh wax. Mould the soft wax on to the model with the fingers.

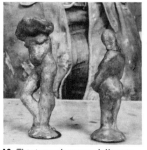

13. This type of wax modelling is used for small models. Wax can also be modelled on to a core of a different material.

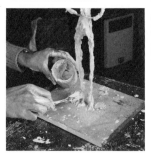

4. Mix a small amount of plaster and apply with a metal tool to work up the detail. For fine detail, use smaller tools.

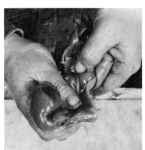

6. Knead the wax into a malleable ball. Work it vigorously until it is the correct texture.

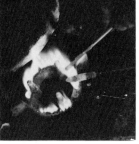

10. Tools for wax modelling can be heated in a flame. Check whether the tool can be left in the flame or just passed through it briefly.

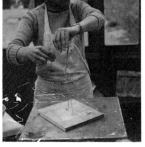

Modelling direct in plaster
1. Make a wire armature and bend it into an appropriate shape.

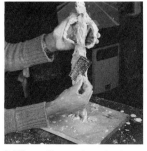

5. When sufficient plaster has been added, shape with a Surform blade to remove excess plaster and complete the detail work.

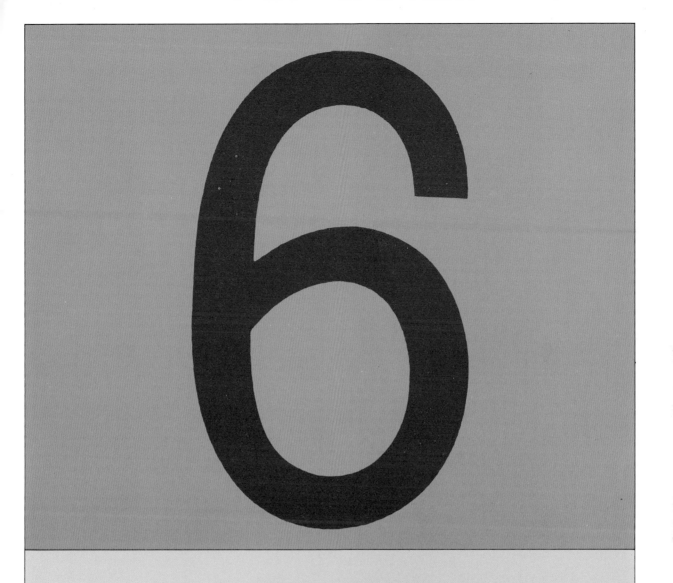

Casting.

History. Suitable subjects. Casting moulds: Clay, Plaster of Paris, Cire perdue. **Filling moulds:** Bronze, Other metals, Plaster of Paris, Polyester resins, Liquid clay.

Casting History

T he basic principles of casting have not changed since the Bronze Age when tools and weapons were made from an open mould carved out of rock. The molten metal was poured into the mould and allowed to set. This technique was universally used by early civilizations and the methods and materials are still being developed today.

The earliest known bronze dates from c.5000 BC, although cast bronze tools were not in general use for another 3,000 to 3,500 years. The first Egyptian bronze casts appeared several hundred years later and Egyptian casting was at its best during the Saite dynasty (c.600 BC). Works of this period include the statue of Horus, in the Louvre.

The ancient Greeks used bronze extensively for casting small statuettes, and this practice was later extended to larger works. Like many early civilizations they used sand as a mould, as well as developing the cire perdue ('lost wax') method of casting from wax.

Although casting was used in Africa and China, and in much Roman and early Christian art, it suffered a decline during the Middle Ages and did not really emerge until the early years of the Renaissance in the fourteenth century. By the 1400s Lorenzo Ghiberti (1378–1455), creator of the famous Baptistry doors in Florence, had established a studio and foundry, paving the way for such masters as Donatello (1386–1466) and the Pollaiuollo brothers, Antonio (1432–1498) and Piero (1441–1496).

The influence of the Renaissance was widespread and casting flourished in foundries and studios throughout Europe. By the seventeenth century, cast bronze was being increasingly used in furniture-making, especially in France, where many famous sculptors who used metal casting were later to live and work—among them Auguste Rodin (1840–1917) and Constantin Brancusi (1876–1957).

A more recent development in the history of casting is the use of plaster of Paris. The casts of such antiquities as the towering Trajan column and Michelangelo's David, which can be found in the collection of plaster replicas in London's Victoria & Albert Museum, demonstrate the immense possibilities of plaster casting.

Although traditional casting materials, such as bronze, are still being used, many new ones such as plastic and concrete are being developed. Different ways of using metals have emerged too. The Swiss sculptor, Max Bill (born 1908), and the Briton, Eduardo Paolozzi (born 1924), were among the pioneers of metal-plated bronze casts. The British sculptor Henry Moore (born 1898) was one of the first artists to experiment with cast cement in his architectural sculpture, while plastic and other synthetic materials are widely used for casting in all art schools.

Suitable subjects

M ost objects and pieces of sculpture can be cast, and the only exceptions are works which are too large to make casting practical or works which involve fine constructions of such materials as thread or wire.

The purpose of casting is to reproduce something in a more permanent, durable material than the original, or to make a number of replicas. Everyday items, or 'found objects', provide unlimited scope for casting, and toys, domestic utensils, stones and pieces of wood are just a few of the objects which have inspired contemporary sculptors.

Casting moulds

The artist has traditionally relied on clay, sand, wax and plaster of Paris for making moulds. Today, however, the choice is wider, encompassing rubber, concrete and plastics, for example. Clay, plaster and polyester are probably the most suitable media for studio casting, especially for the beginner. Metal casting, using either the sand or cire perdue methods, is usually done in a foundry.

Clay

Clay moulds can be made quickly and are suitable for casting plaster, wax or concrete. The master cast should first be dusted with talcum powder or French chalk to prevent sticking. The clay is shaped into fairly thick, flat pieces which are then pressed carefully on to the master cast, the edges fitting closely against each other. The back of the clay should be roughened and each piece reinforced with plaster strengthened with gauze, or scrim. The mould pieces are held in a case which is made by taking a thick plaster and scrim impression of the back of each piece. The mould pieces should first be sealed with shellac and treated with the separating agent. The case sections are then joined together by wooden rods fixed with plaster and scrim, forming a tight-fitting case for the mould.

Plaster of Paris

The two basic types of plaster mould are the waste mould and the piece mould. The method chosen will depend on the material the mould is to be taken from and the number of casts required. The waste mould can only be used once and is suitable for use with a soft object, or master cast, such as wet clay, Plasticine or wax; the piece mould can be used many times and is normally used when the master cast is of a hard substance such as set clay, plaster, plastic or metal.

The waste mould is eventually chipped away from the cast and cannot be re-used. A mould taken from a very simple master cast will probably only need to be made in two parts—the main part and the cap. The more complicated the master cast the more caps will be required on the mould, as the caps enable the modelling material of the master cast to be removed.

For a simple shape requiring a two-piece mould a

line is drawn on the master cast to mark the division between the main mould and the cap. The division can be made by building a clay wall using strips of clay about half an inch (1.25cm) wide. The cap is made first, the strips being laid along the dividing line leaving a clean edge on the cap side. These walls can be reinforced with clay supports on the other side. Alternatively, the mould can be divided by using brass strips, or shims. These are inserted evenly into the master cast along the dividing line making a continuous wall at least half an inch (1.25cm) high. The shims can be cut to fit the shape of the master cast.

Small quantities of plaster are mixed at a time to avoid waste, and this is built up in layers on the cap. Care should be taken not to cover the top of the clay dividing wall and the first coat of plaster should be coloured with a warning dye. When the cap is dry the clay wall is removed and the plaster edge treated with a separating agent such as wax or grease. The main part of the mould is made in the same way after which at least an hour is allowed for the plaster to dry. The mould is then soaked in water and gently parted along the join. Both pieces are then cleaned and treated with the separating agent before use.

The piece mould, as its name suggests, is made in any number of pieces which are supported and held together by a mould case. This method requires patience and practice, and can be used only when the master cast is made of a hard substance. The main advantage of the piece mould is that it can be used many times over.

The surface of a porous master cast, such as plaster, must be sealed with shellac and then treated with the separating agent. To make a simple piece mould of three parts—the main piece and two caps—the dividing lines are drawn on to the master cast.

The side of the master cast which will eventually form the main piece of the mould is firmly embedded in a platform of clay and a wide clay band fitted round it about a quarter of an inch (0.6cm) below the dividing line. Plaster is then built up on top of this, up to the dividing line, a small neat gap being left between the plaster and the master cast. The plaster is then trimmed and treated with the separating agent. The small gap is filled with clay to mark the seam line.

A clay wall is then built between the two caps and enough plaster mixed to make one of them. When this cap has been formed with plaster, the clay wall is removed and the separating agent applied to the new plaster edge. The second cap is then made in the same way.

Before the work is turned to make the main mould piece, a case is made to hold the two complete caps. This is done by applying the separating agent to the backs of the caps and building up a thick plaster covering. When this is hardened, the whole work is turned over, the bands of clay and plaster removed, and the main mould piece made. The third mould piece is thicker than the caps and does not need to have a case.

Polyester resins
Polyester can be used to make a cast that is both strong and light. The method is very similar to the piece mould, one of the basic types of plaster mould. A porous master cast must be sealed with shellac followed by a wax polish. The seam walls are built up with Plasticine and the mould pieces are built up with resin reinforced with glass fibres cut to the right length. Resin painted on to the master cast, forms the first layer. As resin can be drilled the seams can be held together with bolts.

Resin must be mixed before use with a catalyst to harden it, an accelerator to speed up the hardening and a filler to make it less runny. Quantities and types of these resin additives vary and the manufacturer's instructions should be followed.

Cire perdue
This ancient method of casting metal from a wax positive is a job for the professional founder. The original master cast can be of any material but a wax positive must always be made from this. Most types of mould are suitable for this, although one of the flexible types is usually selected.

Melted wax is painted in a thin layer on the inside of the mould to ensure accurate reproduction of fine detail. The mould is then put together and filled with wax. This is poured out leaving a thin deposit of wax on the inside of the mould. The process is repeated several times until the correct thickness has been achieved. The wax positive is then ready and the mould can be taken off. The seam marks are removed at this stage. The hollow wax positive is then filled with a core of porous clay, or another fireproof substance, which is held in position by metal rods.

The wax positive is fitted with a system of runners and risers, a series of tubes through which the molten metal will eventually run and the hot gases rise. At this stage they are wax rods joined on to the positive; when the wax has melted, however, they become hollow spaces in the finished mould. A hole is left at the base of the work through which to pour the hot metal.

The wax positive is then ready for its final coat, or investment, which is usually made of plaster of Paris mixed with ground ceramic. The first layer is painted finely on to the wax and the remainder built up into a thick covering. When dry, the whole investment is heated until the wax has melted and run out through one of the runners which has been extended through the investment. Before the molten metal is poured into the runner system, the specially extended runner must be plugged and the whole investment reinforced by being buried in sand.

Materials for casting
Casting materials include plaster
(**1**), modelling clay (**2**), French
chalk (**3**), separating agent (**4**),
polyester resin (**5**), red wax (**6**),
glass fibre (**7**), plasticine (**8**) and
builder's sand (**9**). Various types
and grades of plaster are
available, experiment and find
which suits your purposes best; a
fine grade of plaster is best for
making a plaster cast. Dental or
medical plaster is suitable. In
addition to clay, slip (liquid clay)
is sometimes needed. To make this,
mix finely ground clay with water
to a creamy consistency. French
chalk is used as a separating
agent, talcum powder may be
used instead. Glass fibre is
used to strengthen the cast at
different stages, particularly in the
resin casting process. Builder's
sand is used in the foundry for
filling the pit in which the mould is
placed, before it is cast into metal.

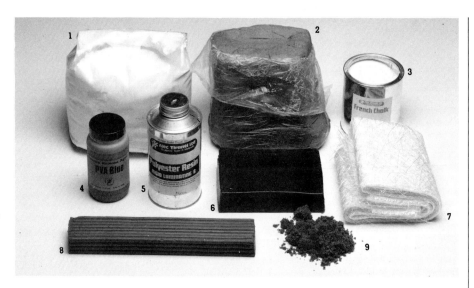

Casting Filling moulds

Having made the mould with the cast in mind it should be noted that each casting material has its own properties and special problems.

Bronze
Whether cast in sand or by the cire perdue method, bronze casting is normally carried out in a foundry. The bronze is melted in a furnace to a temperature of about 1880°F (1010°C). The molten metal is poured quickly into the mould before it starts to cool.

Other metals
Most metals are cast in a foundry. With the exception of lead, metals cannot be poured directly into a mould because of the gases given off forming bubble holes in the finished cast. Casting temperatures for different metals vary considerably. Gold and silver, like bronze, require a casting temperature of about 1880°F (1010°C). Lead, however, requires a much lower temperature and can be melted in an iron saucepan over a cooker. Because it does not give off gases when hot, lead does not need the complex system of runners and risers which other metals require. This makes lead a popular studio metal, but it should be noted that it is subject to some shrinkage during cooling.

Plaster of Paris
For a solid plaster casting, a plaster mould should be lined with soft soap or detergent. As plaster of Paris dries quickly, a sufficient quantity should be mixed to fill the mould. This should be poured gently until the mould is full; the mould should be moved a little during pouring to help release air bubbles. When the plaster has set the mould should be turned upright to allow the plaster to drain, and left for at least an hour.

Polyester resins
Resins are the most common plastics used for casting. The cast is usually hollow and built up against the mould using glass fibre for reinforcement. Only the very smallest objects can be cast in resin by the pouring method.

Many mould materials are suitable for casting from in resin, including plaster of Paris, rubber and resin itself. The separating agent varies for different resins, but Polyvinyl Alcohol (PVA) is generally suitable. The first one or two layers of resin, made up according to the manufacturer's instructions, are painted on. The glass fibres are cut to fit the mould and built up to the required thickness with more resin.

Liquid clay
Slip, or liquid clay, is ideally suited to a porous mould such as plaster of Paris. The slip is poured into the mould which absorbs the water from the slip, leaving a sediment of thick clay around the mould. The longer the slip is left in the mould, the thicker the layers of sediment will be. When the correct thickness is achieved the thin clay should be poured away and the hollow clay cast allowed to harden before the mould is taken out.

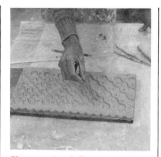

Clay pressing 1. Press a pattern into a sheet of rolled out clay. This simple form of casting can be used for making jars or vases.

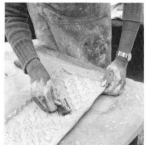

5. Clean and smooth the plaster using a Surform blade or silicon carbide paper. Brush off excess dust.

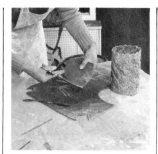

9. Measure and cut out a base from a sheet of wax. Scissors can be used. Paint base with hot wax.

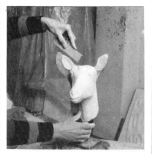

Waste mould 1. Start with a clay model (see previous chapter). Roll out a sheet of clay, cut into strips and make a wall.

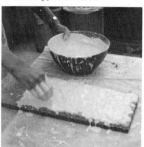

2. Mix some thinnish plaster, flick over the clay bed to cover the pattern. Back up with thicker plaster and make an edge.

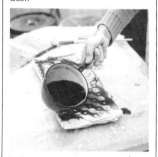

6. Pour melted wax on to the plaster and brush into all the crevices. Allow to set.

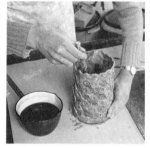

10. Put body firmly on the base. Fill in joints with hot wax. The wax can now be sent to the foundry for casting.

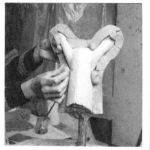

2. Place the wall along the centre of the model. Add pieces of clay to support the wall which will divide the two halves of the mould.

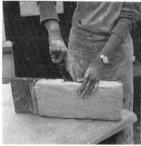

3. Take the clay sheet and plaster mould off the backing when the plaster has set.

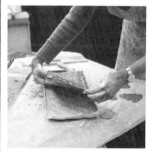

7. Peel off the wax carefully. Wax does not adhere to wet plaster. Bend the wax sheet round to form a vase.

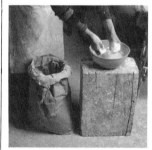

Mixing plaster 1. Sprinkle plaster over the surface of water in a bowl until the plaster is just below the water surface.

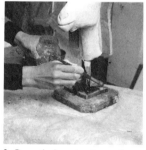

3. Cover the board and any other areas to which the plaster is not to adhere with grease or oil.

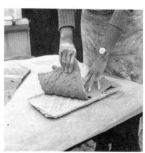

4. Lift the clay off the plaster. Try not to leave any clay on the plaster surface.

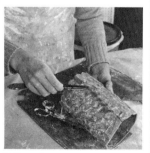

8. Tie with wire or an elastic band. Trim excess wax off the edge. Firm up joint with a hot tool.

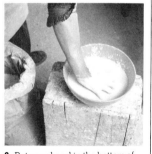

2. Put your hand in the bottom of the bowl and shake gently to mix the plaster. Do not make the plaster too thick .

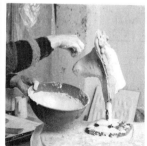

4. Add a little blue colour to the first coat of plaster. Flick the plaster on so that it covers the whole surface thinly.

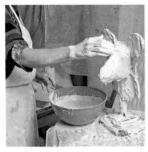

5. Apply a second thicker coat of plaster. Build up plaster gradually with a wiping movement. Build up the edges.

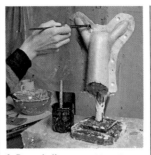

9. Paint shellac on joint to act as separating agent. Repeat steps 4 and 5 to complete the waste mould.

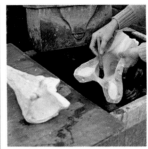

13. Wash out the mould in cold water until it is completely clean. Clay will stain the cast so remove carefully with a brush.

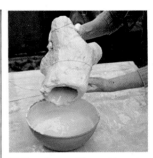

17. Turn the mould round to coat the whole surface, especially any crevices. Build up thickness of the cast to at least 1in (2.5cm).

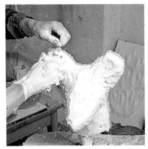

6. When the plaster is slightly dry, cut back on the edges with a knife to reveal the clay wall.

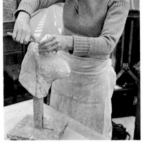

10. Scrape back the completed waste mould with a knife to reveal the shellac-painted joint.

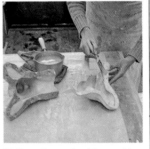

14. Paint the inside of the mould with a separating agent, a weak solution of washing soda (sodium carbonate) and water.

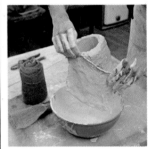

18. Where necessary, reinforce the back of the cast with scrim which has been dipped in the plaster.

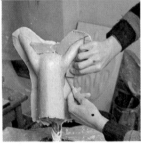

7. Remove the wall by peeling off the clay. Be careful not to damage the plaster.

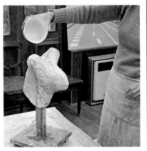

11. Pour water over the seam to swell the clay inside and help separate the joint. Prise the two halves apart with a blunt chisel.

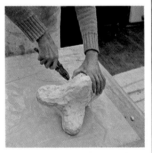

15. Put the 2 halves of the mould together and tie together tightly with thin galvanized binding wire.

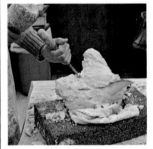

19. When the plaster cast has set, undo the wires and chip away the plaster mould down to the blue coating.

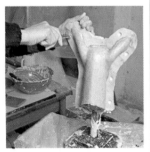

8. Make locating — or key — holes in the plaster with the rounded end of a knife. The holes should be about ¼in (6mm) deep.

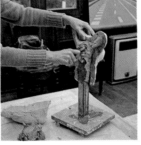

12. Dig the clay out of the mould with a wire tool.

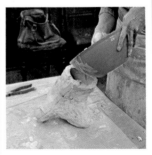

16. Mix plaster to the consistency of thin cream. Pour into the mould.

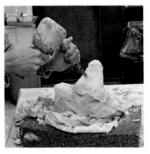

20. Chip the exposed blue coat away. Be careful not to damage the cast underneath.

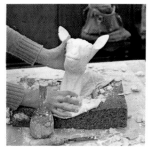

21. Continue to chip away at the blue coat until the finished plaster cast emerges.

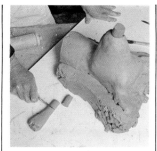

4. Cut a roll of clay into small pieces, the 'chimneys'. Place on the nose and ears. Add a strip of clay around the edge.

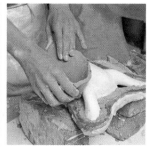

8. Take off the top half of the case and remove all the clay including the chimneys from the case and the original.

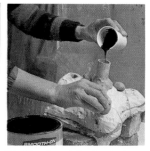

12. When the solution begins to come out of the holes, block them with the clay balls. Allow to cool. Repeat for the other side.

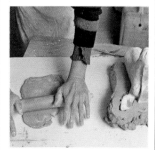

Flexible mould 1. Take the finished plaster cast. Roll out a ½in (1.25cm) thick sheet of clay.

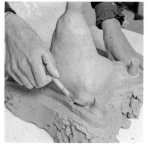

5. Key in with a wire tool. Cover with plaster, allow to dry. Remove from clay bed and turn over. Repeat for the other side.

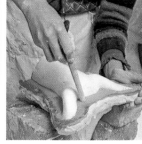

9. Smooth down the dividing layer and add keyholes.

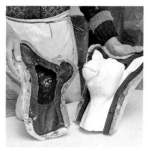

13. Take the halves of the mould apart. No separating agent is required. The finished mould can be used many times.

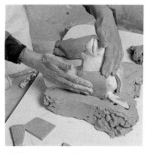

2. Cut out strips of clay and press on to the cast. Repeat until the whole of the cast is covered.

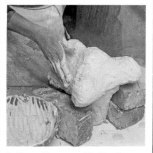

6. Cover the second half with plaster. Allow to dry. A flexible mould has the advantage that it can be reused.

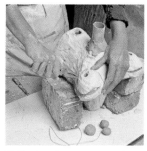

10. Replace the case, tie together with wire, add the funnel and make clay balls.

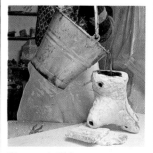

Wax cast 1. Melt wax, pour it into the mould inside the case. Allow to cool. When the wax is about 1/8in (3mm) thick, pour the rest back.

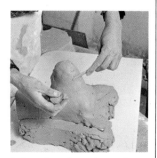

3. Smooth out the surface with a modelling tool or your fingers. The clay represents the rubber compound of the flexible mould.

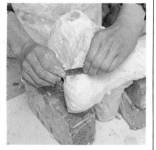

7. Using a knife, scrape back the plaster so that the chimneys show through clearly.

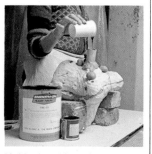

11. Mix the rubber solution according to the manufacturer's instructions. Pour into the funnel.

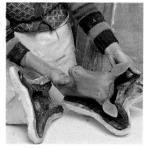

2. When the wax has cooled, take the mould apart carefully, revealing the wax cast, which can be sent for casting into metal.

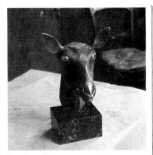

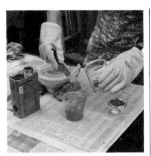

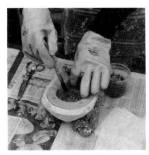

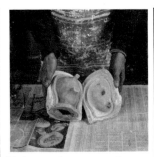

Casting Casting in metals such as bronze is not a studio process; it must be done in a foundry. For the cire perdue or lost wax process, the sculptor provides the foundry with either a wax positive, such as can be made from a flexible mould, or a plaster master cast from which the foundry produces a wax positive. The wax is filled with a core of porous clay held in place by metal rods. Next, a series of tubes called the runners and risers are fitted, through which the molten metal will be poured and the gases will rise. The final coat of plaster, the investment, is added, the whole is heated, the wax runs out, leaving a space into which the metal is poured. Lastly, the cast is finished by the sculptor. Casting in resin is a more recently developed cold process which can be done in the studio.

3. Make the resin solution exactly according to the manufacturer's instructions. Add metal powder and mix thoroughly.

7. Paint in resin, place the strips one at a time in the mould and stipple in to place. Make sure there are no air bubbles.

11. Remove the wire, open the mould and take the case off one half at a time. Take care not to damage either the case or mould.

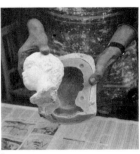

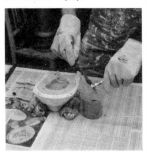

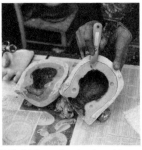

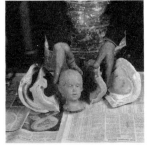

Resin casting 1. For resin casting, start with a flexible mould in its case. Take out the master cast.

4. Add the exact amount of hardener and mix well. Treat the resin materials with great caution as they are highly toxic.

8. Build the cast up to about ¼in (6mm) in thickness. Trim off excess resin. Repeat process for the other half.

12. With great care, remove the one half of the mould from the cast. Repeat for the other half.

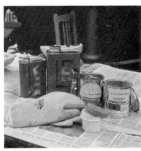

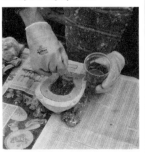

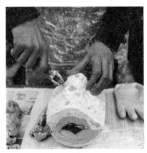

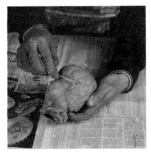

Resin casting 1. continued...

5. Paint the first or 'gel' coat in to the mould. Cover all cracks and crevices. Leave for about 25 minutes to set.

9. When the resin has set, place the 2 halves together and tie with wire.

13. Clean up the seam and remove any excess resin. Use a riffler for small works or power tools for large scale pieces.

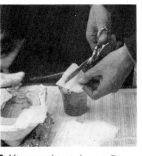

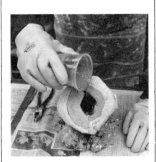

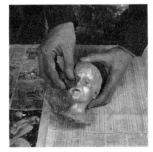

2. Resin casting equipment includes brush cleaner, resin, pre-gel paste, catalyst, gloves, barrier cream, metal powder.

6. Mix second coat of resin. Cut thin strips of glass fibre. These will be used to reinforce the cast.

10. Mix more resin with metal powder and pour in to the joint. Make sure that it goes all round the joint. Allow to set.

14. With wire wool, buff up the cast to bring out the metallic sheen.

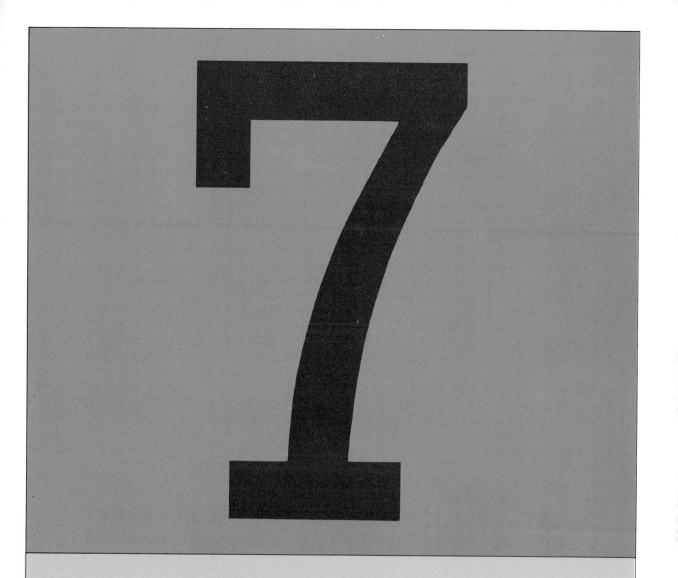

Metal sculpture.

History. Types of metal: Aluminium, Brass, Copper, Iron, Steel. **Tools. Techniques:** Welding, Annealing, Tempering, Soldering, Riveting, Painting to prevent rust, Finishing.

Metal sculpture History

The art of direct metal sculpture, as opposed to metal casting, belongs essentially to modern times with a large proportion of all contemporary sculpture using metal of some kind.

Although some of the metal-sculpting techniques were known to ancient man, they were employed mainly in craft work such as the hammering and beating of armour and the carving and engraving of jewellery.

The metal-workers of ancient Egypt beating sheets of gold over a carved wooden form and the Roman craftsmen hammering out bronze masks clearly have direct links with skilled metal-workers today. Modern artists use the forging techniques of the blacksmith, the carving and engraving skills of the jeweller, and the welding and riveting processes of the shipbuilder.

The discovery of oxyacetylene welding in 1895 brought many new possibilities and scope for sculptors, both in scale and technique. The first artist to exploit this innovation was the Spaniard Julio González (1876–1942). His welded work appeared in 1927 and he later passed on his skill to Picasso (1881–1973).

Many artists were quick to realize metal's positive qualities as a sculpting medium: it can be cut, welded, moulded, cast, polished or patinated and the final result is of a durability that surpasses all but the hardest stones. By the 1940s many of those artists experimenting with welded metal, such as the American sculptor David Smith (1906–1965), were achieving recognition. Within another ten years the art of metal sculpture was firmly established, a development which is demonstrated clearly in the works of such British artists as Anthony Caro (born 1924), Alexander Calder (1898–1976) and Lynne Chadwick (born 1914).

Metal sculpture Types of metals

The experienced metal-worker is aware of the qualities of each of the different metals, notably their malleability, ductility (how easily they can be drawn out into wire) and, of course, availability and expense. Most metals can be bought in bars, sticks, rods, tubes or sheets.

Aluminium
This very satisfactory welding metal is difficult to model because it loses form completely when heated.

Brass
This copper and zinc alloy is commonly used for welding, but care must be taken to avoid inhaling the poisonous fumes which are released. Brass is malleable, takes a high polish and resists corrosion.

Copper
A malleable and ductile metal, copper combines well to make other metals such as brass and bronze. It is unaffected by water or steam, but it reacts with oxygen in the air and turns green.

Iron
Pure iron rusts readily and it is becoming increasingly rare in sculpture. Alloys are more common, and wrought-iron is frequently used because the smelting process makes it tougher than pure iron. Wrought-iron is malleable, ductile and easily welded.

Steel
Of the wide variety of steels, some are too hard and brittle to work. Stainless steel, for instance, is difficult to model but comparatively easy to join; mild steel is one of the most popular for welding.

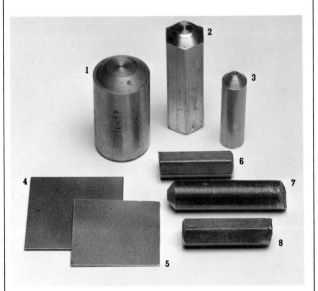

Types of metal It is important for the sculptor to be aware of the qualities of the metal which he or she is going to use. Aluminium, for example, is available in the form of hexagonal bars (**2,6**) or cylindrical bars (**3, 1**) of different sizes. Among the more popular metals for sculpture are copper (**4**) and brass (**5**), here in sheet form. A wide range of steels are manufactured, but many may be too hard or brittle to work. Like aluminium, steel is made in the form of cylindrical (**7**) or hexagonal (**8**) bars, as well as sheets or rods. Mild steel is the most popular form for welding.

Metal sculpture Tools and techniques

Tools for metal sculpture
Working in metal requires a range of specialized equipment. An engineer's vice (**8**) is an essential piece of basic equipment. It should be firmly fastened to a work bench. An anvil is also a useful piece of equipment; a small model (**9**) can be used on a work bench, but a larger version can have additional attachments such as a swage, which is used with molten metal. The range of hammers needed includes a sledge hammer (**1**) for heavy work, a hide hammer (**3**) which does not damage the surface of the metal, a scaling or chipping hammer (**4**) for chipping away at a welded joint and a ball pein hammer (**5**). Among the wrenches used in metal working are a small and large adjustable wrench (**2**) and a self-locking, adjustable plier wrench (**7**). A choice of chisels, including small and large (**6**), is also vital.

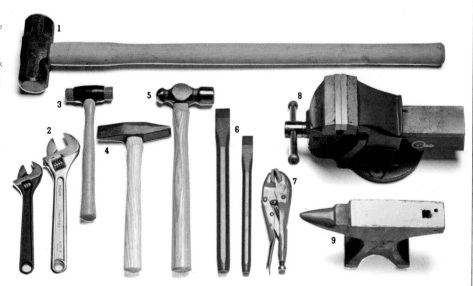

Welding
Any means of fusing metals is known as welding, and it is normally done by arc-welding which requires a sustained electrical discharge or by flame-welding using oxyacetylene.

Oxyacetylene, a combination of oxygen and acetylene, is the most common source of energy for the heat, although other gases can be used. The welder's torch, or flame, is run along the two pieces to be joined until the metals melt and fuse.

Arc-welding is quicker than flame-welding but it is less versatile. The process is most often used for welding steel; it is unsuitable for modelling and detailed work because of the intense heat and light and the necessity to wear cumbersome protective clothing which hinders access to the work.

Annealing
This is an industrial means of heat-treating metals to make them more easily workable when cold. Annealing also corrects stresses inherent within the metal. The temperature to which it should be heated varies according to the type of metal but should not be hot enough to change its structure. Copper may be cooled in cold water after heating. Other metals should be allowed to cool more slowly in the air.

Soldering
A join which will not be required to take any strain can be executed with soft solder, an alloy of lead and tin, which has a very low melting-point. Hard solder always contains a high proportion of the metal being worked on and has a higher melting-point. Both types of soldering require the metals to be cleaned with a

flux first; this is a solvent which is painted on to the cleaned surface to dissolve dirt and grease, thus enabling the solder to take properly.

Tempering
Steel can be brought to a required degree of hardness and elasticity by the process known as tempering. The term is usually applied to tool steels, which are heated to a specific temperature before being quickly immersed in cold water.

Riveting
Holes for rivets can be drilled or punched. The rivets can be countersunk, and the subsequent filling and grinding down make them completely invisible. Rivet joins are permanent; for removable joins, bolts and screws can be used.

Painting to prevent rust
Proprietary paint finishes can be clear or coloured and are always sprayed on to the work in a succession of thin coats rather than brushed. The surface of the work should first be rubbed down with an abrasive to provide a key for the paint.

Alternatively, rusting can be prevented by spraying the model with particles of a rust-resistant metal, such as zinc.

Finishing
Most metals can be coloured by chemicals: copper and brass, for example, turn green when bathed in a solution of hot copper nitrate. Steel turns black if it is subjected to a jet of steam when red-hot.

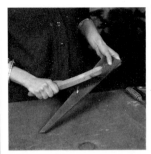

Welding 1. To prepare the surface of the metal, brush off excess rust with a wire brush.

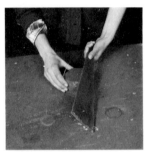

2. Place the edges which are to be welded together. Welding at the edge gives a stronger joint.

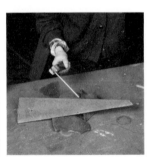

3. Before beginning to weld, balance and, if necessary, support the pieces so they are steady. Clamps can also be used.

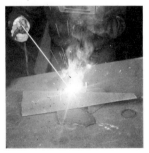

4. Weld the edges by weaving the flow of molten steel from the electrode across the edges.

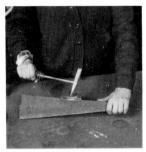

5. Remove balancing pieces or clamps and, wearing safety goggles, chip off excess slag with a chipping hammer.

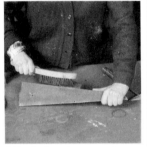

6. Brush along the joint to clear off the slag. The electrode consists of an outer coat of slag and the steel core which is melted.

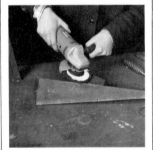

Using the grinder 1. The grinder is used to clean the joint up. Goggles should be worn because of the dust.

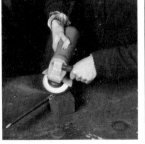

2. The grinder must be held with great care to ensure that it stays steady. The grinder can also be used to remove a faulty weld.

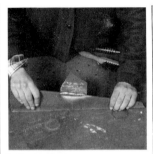

3. The finished seam should be shiny in appearance.

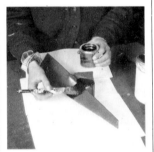

Priming 1. After preparing the metal, paint on a first coat of red or white oxide primer. For large areas use a mask in case of fumes.

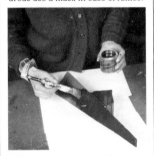

2. Two coats of primer will normally suffice. White primer oxide is better if coloured paint is to be used to finish the surface.

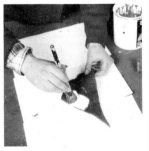

Painting 1. Apply one coat of emulsion paint to the primed surface.

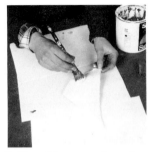

2. After adding a second coat of paint, apply a coat of matt polyurethane varnish to protect the surface.

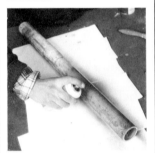

3. Spray paint can also be used. It is hard-wearing and comes in a wide variety of colours.

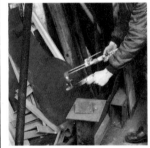

Cutting 1. An oxyacetylene torch can be used to cut through metal. It should only be used under close supervision.

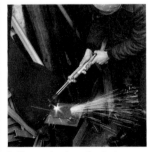

2. The torch is lit with a flick gun. Stringent safety precautions are vital when using this equipment.

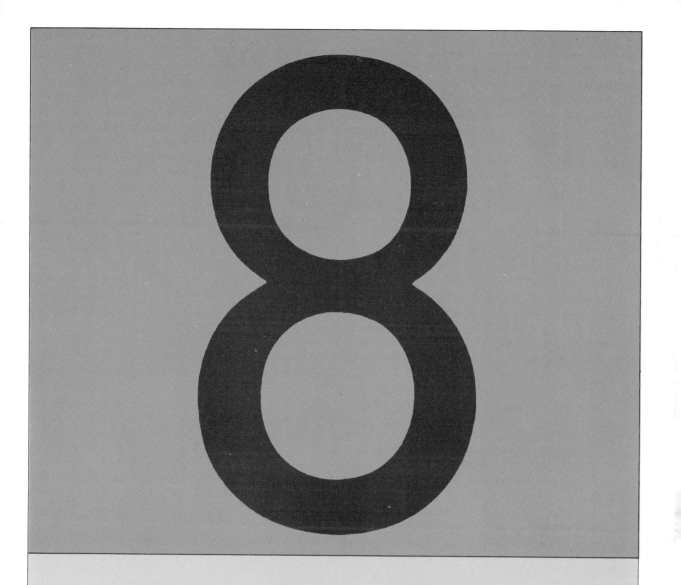

Sculpture with Perspex.

History and materials. Techniques and equipment: Cutting, Heat forming, Annealing, Joining and glueing, Wet sanding, Laminating, Drawing and painting, Engraving and lighting, Polishing and cleaning. **Tools and equipment.**

Perspex History and materials

The concept of heavy monumental forms was revolutionized by two Russian-born brothers, later known as Constructivists, Antoine Pevsner (1886–1962) and Naum Gabo (1890–1977) in their Realist Manifesto. They claimed that sculpture should be light, airy and transparent. László Moholy-Nagy (1895–1946), who taught at the *Bauhaus* from 1923–1928, worked almost exclusively with plexiglass acrylic sheets, heating and forming them into multi-dimensional shapes. Gabo and Moholy-Nagy during the 1940s were the first exponents of transparent sculptures of heat-shaped acrylic.

Plastics, which are capable of permanent change in shape by the application of heat or pressure, are divided into two basic groups: thermoplastic and thermosetting. Thermoplastic resins, which are discussed here, soften whenever they are exposed to sufficient heat and harden when cool; they will continue to do so no matter how often the process is repeated.

Thermoplastic materials such as acrylic sheet may be heated and formed into many different three-dimensional shapes. They can be bonded together to make opaque or transparent architectural sculpture.

The clear quality of acrylic sheet, sometimes known as plastic glass, refracts more than glass. Acrylic resins, developed in the 1930s, are only half as heavy as glass, and much stronger in impact resistance; the surface is softer, however, and is easily damaged by abrasion. Acrylic sheets do not shrink or deteriorate and are reasonably resistant to most domestic chemicals. They are little affected by exposure to water or moisture, but they are not impervious to lower alcohols and aromatic solvents such as turpentine, benzene, toluene, lacquer thinner, acetone and ketone.

Acrylic sheets are cast by pouring thick acrylic casting syrup between sheets of plate glass, and are made in different surface patterns and textures. Coloured sheets are obtained by adding pigments or dyes to the casting monomer.

Sheets are made in shrunk or unshrunk acrylic. The unshrunk form is cheaper, but, when heated for forming, shrinks by about 2.2% in length and increases by about 4% in thickness. Shrunk sheets remain stable when heated. Commercially available plastics include Acrylite and Oroglas in the United States, Perspex in England and Altuglas in France.

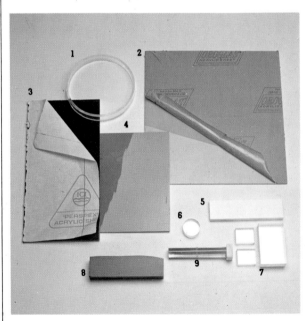

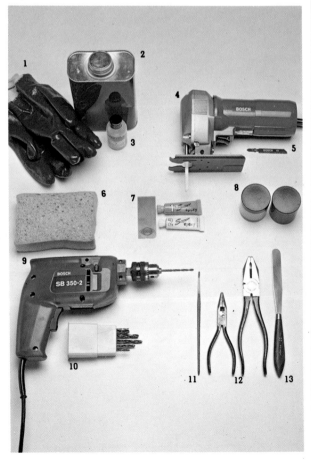

Types Sheet acrylic is available in different forms, translucencies and colours. These can be used separately or in combination. The range includes clear acrylic sheet in the form of cylinders (**1**), rods (**9**) and sheets of varying thicknesses (**6**,**7**). The colours available include brown (**3**), orange (**4**) and turquoise (**2**), opaque white (**5**) and black (**8**).

Tools and equipment Working with acrylic sheet demands certain fairly specialized tools and equipment. These include a power drill (**9**) and bits (**10**), electric jigsaw (**4**) and tungsten carbide blade (**5**), acrylic monomer (**2**) and catalyst (**3**), epoxy resin adhesive and spatula (**7**), dyes (**8**). Also useful are a sponge (**6**), brush (**11**), pliers (**12**), palette knife (**13**) and protective gloves (**1**).

Perspex Techniques and Equipment

crylic sheets can be readily sawn, heat-shaped, drilled with a carbide-tipped drill piece or with purpose-made drill pieces, using oil or soapy water as a lubricant. They can also be cemented, sanded, coloured and polished.

Cutting
A table saw with a fine-toothed tungsten carbide cutting blade is adequate; the acrylic sheet is fed slowly through the saw to avoid too much heat caused by friction. Red sealing-wax, beeswax or even soap will keep the blade lubricated. Safety goggles should be worn to avoid particles of acrylic dust.

Heat forming or shaping
When acrylic sheets are heated to about 250°F (103°C) they become soft and pliable. Smaller pieces can be heated in a kitchen stove or with an electric burner or blowtorch. Acrylic sheet will edge-ignite if heated over 700°F (371°C), and interesting effects can be produced if it is deliberately ignited and put out.

Annealing
Tempering or toughening, known as annealing, is carried out by slowly and gradually decreasing heat. Annealing helps to reduce internal stresses which may have arisen during machining or heating.

Joining and glueing
A solvent cement is best for joining acrylic sheets. Ethylene dichloride can be applied to both the cleaned and smoothed surfaces with an eye-dropper, brush or syringe. The surfaces to be joined are softened by the solvent, and the result is a strong, transparent join.

Different materials can be joined to acrylic sheets with epoxy cements. Duco all-purpose cement, for example, can be used to glue loose materials or glass fragments called tesserae to clear acrylic sheet when making a transparent collage or mosaic; catalyzed clear polyester is then poured over the mosaic to bind the loose materials together.

Wet sanding
The best results are obtained with garnet or aluminium oxide abrasive papers. Light surface sanding provides a key for better adhesion of acrylic monomer dyes.

Drawing and painting
Transparent and translucent paints and polyester dyes are available for acrylics from specialist craft shops. Dip-dyeing can be used to provide translucent colour.

A Chinagraph pencil is suitable for drawing directly on to the plastic surface, and errors are easily removed with a soft cloth.

Drawings can be traced on the protective paper which comes with the delivered sheet. This remains attached until all the cutting and drilling has been done. A tracing can also be made on a separate piece of paper which is then attached to the protective paper with rubber cement.

Architectural panels with a type of stained glass or mosaic effect can be achieved by drawing on the acrylic sheet with long-tipped tubes of liquid aluminium, steel, lacquer or epoxy-aluminium filled pastes. These form a raised line and the resulting cells are filled with catalyzed clear polyester dye or catalyzed acrylic monomer dyes. As soon as the dye surface sets, it should be left overnight covered with cellophane to exclude air and cause the polyester resin surface to set hard.

Laminating
Acrylic sheets can be sandwiched together with coloured laminating cements which are usually made of high strength solvents. Laminating dye can be applied generously with eye-droppers, spoons or sticks. The second sheet is then laid carefully on top and floated very gently on the wet dye, pressing first from the centre. Care must be taken to avoid bubbles.

Engraving and lighting
Acrylic sheets can be engraved with intaglio designs with burr cutters attached to flexible shaft tools. The surface designs can eventually be illuminated by edge-lighting. Fluorescent lighting tubes along the top or bottom edges of a carved sheet will light up the interior of the plastic and emit light through the engraved pattern.

Polishing and cleaning
Acrylic sculpture should be cleaned only with a mild solution of soap or washing-up liquid and a soft cloth. Anti-static polish can be applied to help prevent dust and particles settling. The final polishing should always be done by hand using a non-scratch cloth, but the sculpture is first buffed with a double-shaft electric buffing machine. One buffer is charged with white tripoli compound to remove scratches, the other with white acrylic compound for final gloss polishing. Only light pressure should be applied or the work may burn as a result of the friction.

Tools and equipment
Most metal-working and wood-carving tools can be used with plastics. As well as the equipment associated with each technique, the following items are required: electric stove burner and a domestic oven (for smaller pieces), hand drill or high speed electric drill with metal bits; electric jig saw with tungsten carbide blades for curved or intricate shapes; pliers, rubber cement, sponges, protective gloves, acrylic monomer and catalyst, dyes, palette knives, brushes, and sticks. Machine tools include lathes, shapers, routers, milling machines, drills and taps.

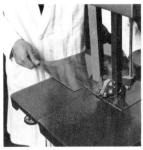

Cutting perspex 1. Perspex is most efficiently cut on a band saw. The perspex should be guided gently through as the blade cuts.

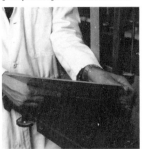

2. The cut edge of the perspex is rough and dusty and will require careful cleaning up before any joining takes place.

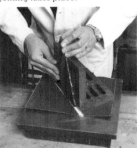

Sandpapering the edges 1. Clamp a piece of sandpaper to a flat surface. Support the perspex at right angles, rub down the edge.

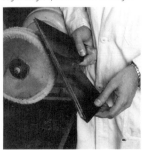

2. The sandpapered edge is now rubbed flat but is still dusty and not completely smooth.

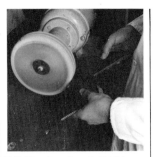

Polishing the edges 1. Hold the edge of the perspex against the rotating wheel of the machine polisher. Keep it moving slightly.

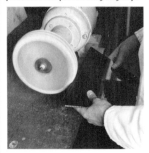

2. Keep the perspex moving slightly. The polisher generates heat so do not hold the perspex too close.

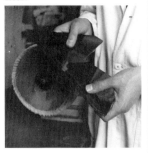

3. The polished edge is smooth and ready for glueing.

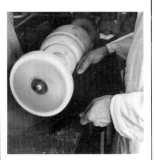

Polishing flat surfaces Hold the flat surface of the perspex against the wheel. Again, keep it moving and not too close.

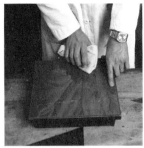

Polishing with a rag As the finished effect of perspex depends upon its sheen and transparency, polishing is a painstaking process.

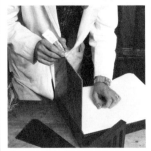

Joining surfaces 1. To join at right angles, apply suitable adhesive to the edge of one piece of perspex.

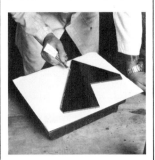

2. Apply adhesive to the edge of the flat surface of the second piece of perspex. Use contact glue and allow it to dry.

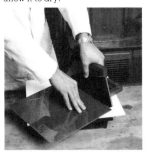

3. Join the glue surfaces together and place the perspex against a right angled support so that a true join is obtained.

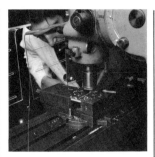

Milling 1. A milling machine can be used to trim perspex or to make slots and grooves in the surface.

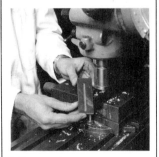

2. The milled groove is even and of uniform depth. Milling can be used as part of the construction process or as surface decoration.

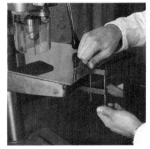

Drilling 1. When drilling perspex, clamp it firmly to the bed of the drill so that it cannot come loose and swivel.

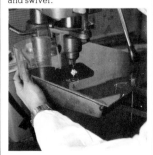

2. Drill the holes carefully and evenly. They can be used to fix two pieces together or to attach perspex to wood or metal.

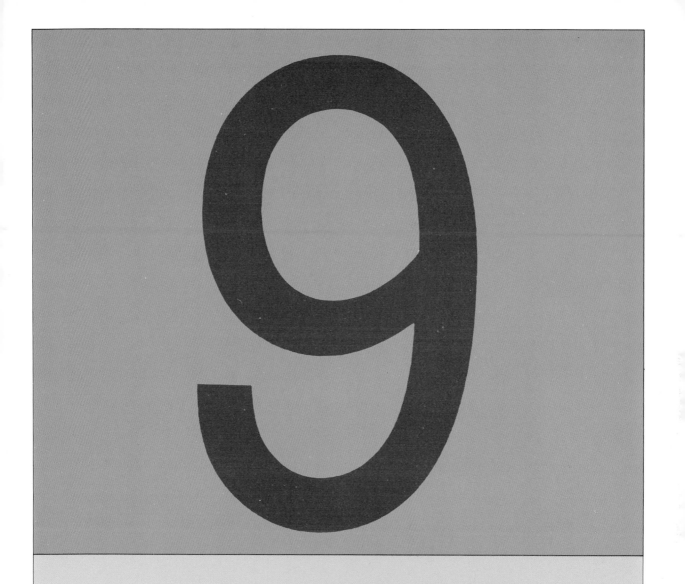

Display and transport.

Transport: Moving large sculptures, Packing a sculpture. **Display:** Outdoor siting, Interior display, Light and space.

Sculpture Transport

A ll types of sculpture, whether small and fragile or heavy and unwieldy, present problems in packing and transporting. If they are to be dismantled and later reassembled, each part should be numbered. A plan or sketch can be drawn to ensure correct assembly, and in some cases a photograph is useful.

One-piece sculptures, such as a stone statue, have to be levered into place with levers and a jack. The sculpture must be protected from the metal tools by pieces of wood.

Large works can be padded with as much soft material—such as blankets—as possible. Corners and projections need special protection. One of the professional methods for packing a piece into a crate requires diagonal struts to be erected between opposite corners of the crate so that they pass through the centre of the cube of space. The piece is then inserted into the crate so that it is supported by the struts, and soft materials are then packed around it to absorb jolts.

When lifting by hand, canvas or leather slings are ideal for works which are not too large. Gloves should be worn to protect the work from grease marks and to protect the lifter from any sharp material.

Stone works, particularly, can be moved by means of a pulley in the studio. One of the common systems uses three pulleys. A low trolley with small, strong wheels, known as a sampson, is often used for moving heavy works. The sculpture is usually levered into place.

Monumental stone works are usually transported by crane or forklift truck. They must be well protected and secured with ropes; the sculptures can then be guided into place by hand.

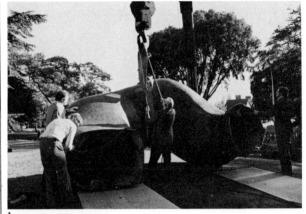

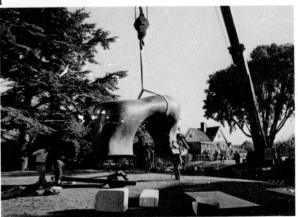

1

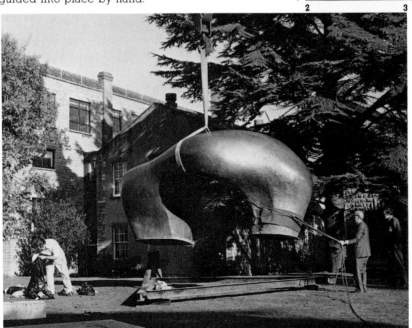

2   3   4

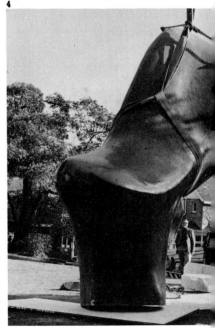

Transporting sculpture These pictures (**left**) show the British sculptor, Henry Moore, supervising the siting of his large sculpture *Sheep Piece* in an outdoor setting in Street, Somerset, England. This sculpture consists of two pieces, each of which had to be moved individually. For moving large pieces of sculpture a crane may be necessary (**1**). However, it is vital that the sculpture is kept in balance and that the surface is not damaged. The sculpture will eventually stand on a triangular base (**2**) which will be buried in the ground. Before this can be done, the exact positioning of the sculpture has to be checked (**3**). Note how the sculpture is guided by being pulled with a rope. The surface is protected by a guard made of soft material. As a safety precaution, a chain is added for moving the second and larger piece of the sculpture (**4**).

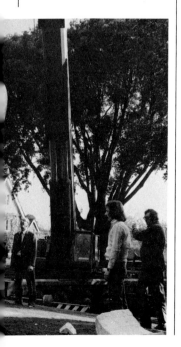

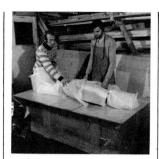

Packing a sculpture for transport
1. A crate is specially made to a suitable size. The sculpture is first wrapped in tissue paper.

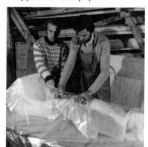

2. The sculpture is then wrapped completely in polythene sheeting which is firmly secured with adhesive tape.

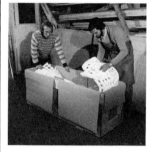

3. Corrugated cardboard is laid in the crate and then padded cushions of paper stuffed with straw are laid in as a bed.

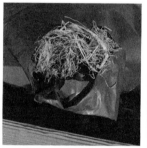

4. Thick layers of foam rubber are placed over the bed and are allowed to hang over the sides of the crate.

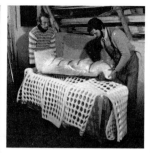

5. The wrapped sculpture is placed in the crate on the foam rubber bed. Using waste pieces and offcuts can save expense.

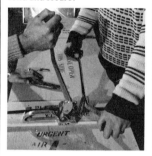

6. The overhanging foam is tightly packed around the sculpture in the crate and another layer added on top and tucked into the sides.

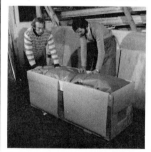

7. More paper parcels stuffed with straw are laid on top and pressed firmly down on to the rest of the packing.

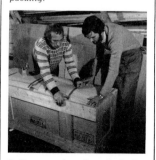

8. Corrugated cardboard is laid over the packing and folded in to the sides of the crate. The inside packing is now complete.

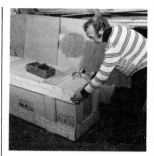

9. The lid of the crate is put in place and nailed down around all four sides so that the crate is quite solid and secure.

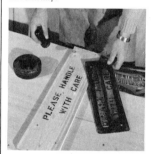

10. Metal bands are passed round the reinforcing battens on the wood crate and are tightened and fixed firmly.

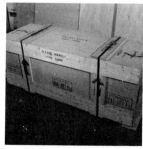

11. Instructions for handling and transporting must be clearly shown on the outside of the crate.

12. The finished package is quite secure and strong, clearly marked with instructions and given added protection by the metal bands.

61

Sculpture Display

E ffective lighting is a crucial factor in the successful display of sculpture and shadows, for example, should be avoided. Ideally, the light should surround the work, rather than emanating from one particular source. The colour of lighting needs thought too—warm light, for instance, can detract from the essentially cold appearance of metal.

The size and shape of the piece dictates its positioning. A piece can be spoilt by being too low so that the top is visible, or too high which produces a distorted view. Plinths should be unobtrusive so as not to detract from the sculpture.

Free-standing works are often mounted on a stand—of stone, metal or wood, for example—and this is carefully chosen to match the sculpture, setting it off in the same way that a frame sets off a picture. The base can be stuck, screwed or nailed to the work, and the bottom can be covered with felt to protect surfaces.

Of vital importance in the display of sculpture outdoors is the 'contrast of line', the lines and outlines not only in the piece itself but also in the environment—the line of the horizon and of the trees and the lines created by buildings. There has to be sufficient space to display the work: two prominent sculptures close together, for example, may detract from one another, whether outdoors or in a gallery.

Atmospheric conditions must be noted as heat and damp, particularly, can have disastrous effects. Many materials, including wood, ferrous metals, chalk and plaster, must be sealed or the pieces will not last. Although soft stones are vulnerable to the elements, stone is usually preferred because of its relative resistance to the weather. However, water-proofing substances are available today for most materials.

Scale and setting In some sculptures the scale of the work, determined in the original conception, may have a vital bearing on the way in which it is displayed. Whereas it is sometimes possible to display sculptures in very different ways, according to whether they are presented in a gallery, private home or out of doors, the two examples shown below contain elements of scale and structure which make a particular type of setting crucial to the work. Anthony Caro's *XLIX* (**below right**) is one of a series of small sculptures which were specially designed to be placed on tables. In this way a range of scale was

fixed from the outset and part of the wholly abstract conception was to emphasize the height of the display in relation to the ground and the table by allowing part of the work to extend over the edge, below the level of the table top. This precludes the possibility of showing the pieces on the ground, as his larger works are displayed, and fixes the relation of the work to its setting. Henry Moore's large scale works are often displayed in the open, in parks or civic settings. The massive scale of his *Arch* (**below**) and its reference to architectural structure make it stand out amongst tall trees and in large open spaces,

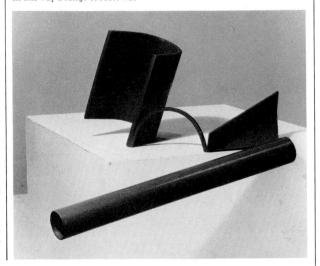

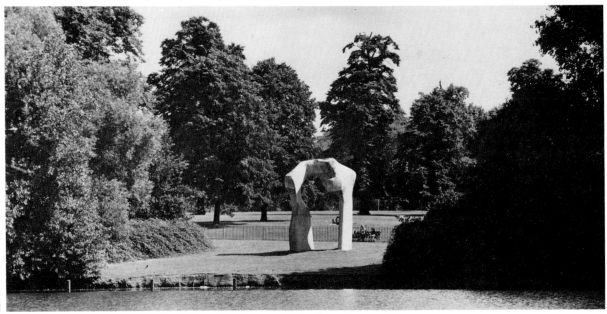